The Book of Zodiac Signs

Crafted by Skriuwer

Table of Contents

6.   **Chapter 1:   Introduction to Astrology and the Zodiac**
- The History and Origins of Astrology
- Understanding the Zodiac: An Overview
- The Zodiac Wheel and Its Significance
- The Four Elements: Fire, Earth, Air, and Water
- The Modalities: Cardinal, Fixed, and Mutable Signs

13.   **Chapter 2:   Aries**
- Aries Overview and Symbolism
- Personality Traits of Aries
- Aries in Love and Relationships
- Career and Ambitions of Aries
- Strengths and Weaknesses of Aries
- Aries Compatibility with Other Signs
- Famous Aries Personalities

24.   **Chapter 3:   Taurus**
- Taurus Overview and Symbolism
- Personality Traits of Taurus
- Taurus in Love and Relationships
- Career and Ambitions of Taurus
- Strengths and Weaknesses of Taurus
- Taurus Compatibility with Other Signs
- Famous Taurus Personalities

34.   **Chapter 4:   Gemini**
- Gemini Overview and Symbolism
- Personality Traits of Gemini
- Gemini in Love and Relationships
- Career and Ambitions of Gemini
- Strengths and Weaknesses of Gemini
- Gemini Compatibility with Other Signs
- Famous Gemini Personalities

45.   **Chapter 5:   Cancer**
- Cancer Overview and Symbolism
- Personality Traits of Cancer
- Cancer in Love and Relationships
- Career and Ambitions of Cancer

- Strengths and Weaknesses of Cancer
- Cancer Compatibility with Other Signs
- Famous Cancer Personalities

57. **Chapter 6:   Leo**
- Leo Overview and Symbolism
- Personality Traits of Leo
- Leo in Love and Relationships
- Career and Ambitions of Leo
- Strengths and Weaknesses of Leo
- Leo Compatibility with Other Signs
- Famous Leo Personalities

68. **Chapter 7:   Virgo**
- Virgo Overview and Symbolism
- Personality Traits of Virgo
- Virgo in Love and Relationships
- Career and Ambitions of Virgo
- Strengths and Weaknesses of Virgo
- Virgo Compatibility with Other Signs
- Famous Virgo Personalities

80. **Chapter 8:   Libra**
- Libra Overview and Symbolism
- Personality Traits of Libra
- Libra in Love and Relationships
- Career and Ambitions of Libra
- Strengths and Weaknesses of Libra
- Libra Compatibility with Other Signs
- Famous Libra Personalities

92. **Chapter 9:   Scorpio**
- Scorpio Overview and Symbolism
- Personality Traits of Scorpio
- Scorpio in Love and Relationships
- Career and Ambitions of Scorpio
- Strengths and Weaknesses of Scorpio
- Scorpio Compatibility with Other Signs
- Famous Scorpio Personalities

103. **Chapter 10: Sagittarius**
- Sagittarius Overview and Symbolism
- Personality Traits of Sagittarius
- Sagittarius in Love and Relationships
- Career and Ambitions of Sagittarius
- Strengths and Weaknesses of Sagittarius
- Sagittarius Compatibility with Other Signs
- Famous Sagittarius Personalities

114 **Chapter 11: Capricorn**
- Capricorn Overview and Symbolism
- Personality Traits of Capricorn
- Capricorn in Love and Relationships
- Career and Ambitions of Capricorn
- Strengths and Weaknesses of Capricorn
- Capricorn Compatibility with Other Signs
- Famous Capricorn Personalities

124. **Chapter 12: Aquarius**
- Aquarius Overview and Symbolism
- Personality Traits of Aquarius
- Aquarius in Love and Relationships
- Career and Ambitions of Aquarius
- Strengths and Weaknesses of Aquarius
- Aquarius Compatibility with Other Signs
- Famous Aquarius Personalities

134. **Chapter 13: Pisces**
- Pisces Overview and Symbolism
- Personality Traits of Pisces
- Pisces in Love and Relationships
- Career and Ambitions of Pisces
- Strengths and Weaknesses of Pisces
- Pisces Compatibility with Other Signs
- Famous Pisces Personalities

144. **Chapter 14: The Influence of the Moon and Rising Signs**
- Understanding the Moon Sign
- How the Moon Sign Affects Personality and Emotions
- The Importance of the Rising Sign (Ascendant)
- How the Rising Sign Influences Appearance and First Impressions

149. **Chapter 15:   The Role of Planetary Aspects and Houses**
- An Introduction to Planetary Aspects
- Major Aspects and Their Meanings
- The Twelve Houses of the Zodiac
- How Planets in Houses Influence Your Life

156. **Chapter 16:   Zodiac Signs and Health**
- Aries to Pisces: Health Strengths and Vulnerabilities
- Tips for Maintaining Wellness Based on Your Zodiac Sign
- Holistic and Astrological Approaches to Health

165. **Chapter 17:   Zodiac Signs in Daily Life**
- How Your Zodiac Sign Influences Your Daily Routine
- Navigating Challenges and Opportunities with Astrology
- Making the Most of Your Zodiac Sign's Strengths

171. **Chapter 18:   Relationships and Compatibility**
- The Dynamics of Zodiac Sign Compatibility
- Love and Romance Compatibility
- Friendship and Family Compatibility
- Working with Different Zodiac Signs

178. **Chapter 19:   Career and Success**
- How Your Zodiac Sign Affects Your Career Choices
- Strategies for Career Success Based on Your Zodiac Sign
- Finding Fulfillment and Balance in Your Professional Life

184. **Chapter 20:   Zodiac Signs and Personal Growth**
- Using Astrology for Personal Development
- Setting Goals and Achieving Growth with Astrological Guidance
- Embracing Your Full Potential Through Understanding Your Zodiac Sign

188. **Chapter 21:   Advanced Astrological Concepts**
- The Role of Retrogrades in Astrology
- Eclipses and Their Impact on the Zodiac
- Understanding and Interpreting Transits

192. **Chapter 22:   Putting It All Together: A Comprehensive Guide**
- How to Read and Interpret Your Birth Chart
- Combining Sun, Moon, and Rising Signs
- Integrating Astrological Insights into Your Life

Chapter 1

Introduction to Astrology and the Zodiac

The History and Origins of Astrology

The history and origins of astrology trace back thousands of years to ancient civilizations such as Mesopotamia, Egypt, and Greece. Astrology is the belief that the positions and movements of celestial bodies, such as planets and stars, can influence human affairs and natural phenomena. The practice of astrology has evolved over time, blending elements of astronomy, philosophy, and spirituality to create a complex system of understanding the cosmos and its impact on individuals.

One of the earliest recorded instances of astrology dates back to ancient Mesopotamia, where astrologers observed the movements of celestial bodies and correlated them with events on Earth. The Babylonians, in particular, developed a sophisticated system of astrology based on the positions of planets in the zodiac. They believed that the movements of the planets could provide insights into the future and help guide decision-making.

In ancient Egypt, astrology was closely tied to the worship of the sun god Ra. Egyptian priests used the positions of the stars and planets to predict agricultural cycles, natural disasters, and the fortunes of the pharaohs. Astrology played a significant role in Egyptian society, influencing everything from religious ceremonies to royal decrees.

The Greeks further developed the practice of astrology, blending it with their philosophical and scientific knowledge. Greek philosophers such as Plato and Aristotle believed that the movements of the celestial bodies could reveal underlying patterns in the universe and help humans better understand their place in the cosmos. Greek astrologers also introduced the concept of the zodiac, a twelve-part division of the sky based on the path of the sun.

Astrology continued to evolve during the Hellenistic period, as Greek knowledge spread to regions such as Persia, India, and the Roman Empire. The famous astrologer Claudius Ptolemy wrote the influential work "Tetrabiblos," which codified many of the astrological concepts still used today. Ptolemy's work laid the foundation for horoscopic astrology, which focuses on interpreting the positions of planets at the time of a person's birth.

During the medieval period, astrology gained popularity in Europe as scholars translated ancient texts and integrated astrological principles into their studies. Astrology was widely practiced among the nobility and clergy, who believed that the movements of the planets could influence political events and personal destinies. Astrologers were consulted for advice on matters ranging from marriage to warfare.

In the modern era, astrology has experienced a resurgence in popularity as people seek guidance and insight into their lives. While some may view astrology as a pseudoscience, others find value in its symbolic and psychological interpretations. Today, astrology is practiced in various forms, including natal chart readings, horoscopes, and compatibility analyses.

Overall, the history and origins of astrology reflect humanity's enduring fascination with the cosmos and our desire to make sense of the world around us. By exploring the ancient roots of astrology, we gain a deeper appreciation for the interconnectedness of the universe and our place within it.

Understanding the Zodiac: An Overview

The Zodiac is a concept deeply rooted in astrology, representing a circle of twelve divisions or signs, each associated with specific traits and characteristics. These signs are based on the position of the sun at the time of a person's birth and are believed to influence their personality, behavior, and destiny. Here is an in-depth overview of the Zodiac and its significance:

1. The Twelve Zodiac Signs:

The Zodiac is divided into twelve signs, each representing a specific period of the year and unique set of qualities. The signs are Aries, Taurus, Gemini, Cancer, Leo, Virgo, Libra, Scorpio, Sagittarius, Capricorn, Aquarius, and Pisces. Each sign is associated with one of the four elements - Fire, Earth, Air, and Water - and falls into one of the three modalities - Cardinal, Fixed, and Mutable.

2. The Elements and Modalities:

The four elements in astrology - Fire, Earth, Air, and Water - play a crucial role in understanding the Zodiac signs. Fire signs (Aries, Leo, Sagittarius) are known for their passion, energy, and creativity. Earth signs (Taurus, Virgo, Capricorn) are grounded, practical, and dependable. Air signs (Gemini, Libra, Aquarius) are intellectual, communicative, and social. Water signs (Cancer, Scorpio, Pisces) are emotional, intuitive, and empathetic.

The modalities further categorize the signs based on their approach to life. Cardinal signs (Aries, Cancer, Libra, Capricorn) are initiators, leaders, and go-getters. Fixed signs (Taurus, Leo, Scorpio, Aquarius) are stable, persistent, and determined. Mutable signs (Gemini, Virgo, Sagittarius, Pisces) are adaptable, flexible, and versatile.

3. The Zodiac Wheel:
The Zodiac wheel is a visual representation of the twelve signs arranged in a circular pattern. The wheel begins with Aries and progresses in a counter-clockwise direction through the signs until it reaches Pisces. Each sign occupies a specific sector of the wheel and is connected to neighboring signs through various astrological relationships.

4. Significance of the Zodiac:
The Zodiac serves as a symbolic framework for understanding human nature and behavior through the lens of astrology. It provides a way to categorize and interpret personality traits, relationships, and life events based on the position of celestial bodies at the time of birth. By studying the Zodiac, individuals can gain insights into themselves and others, as well as navigate life's challenges and opportunities more effectively.

In conclusion, the Zodiac is a fascinating system that offers valuable insights into the complexities of human beings and the universe. By exploring the twelve signs, elements, modalities, and the Zodiac wheel, individuals can deepen their understanding of astrology and its impact on various aspects of life. Embracing the wisdom of the Zodiac can lead to self-discovery, personal growth, and a deeper connection to the cosmic forces that shape our existence.

The Zodiac Wheel and Its Significance
The Zodiac Wheel is a fundamental concept in astrology that plays a crucial role in understanding the characteristics and traits associated with each zodiac sign. The Zodiac Wheel is a circular diagram that represents the division of the sky into twelve equal sections, each corresponding to one of the

zodiac signs. This wheel is divided into 12 segments, with each segment representing a specific zodiac sign that is associated with certain personality traits, characteristics, and qualities.

The Zodiac Wheel is significant because it serves as a symbolic representation of the journey of the Sun through the different zodiac signs over the course of a year. As the Sun travels through each sign, it influences the energy and attributes associated with that particular sign. The Zodiac Wheel helps astrologers track the movement of the Sun and other planets in relation to the zodiac signs, allowing them to make predictions and interpretations about an individual's personality, relationships, and life events.

The twelve signs of the Zodiac Wheel are Aries, Taurus, Gemini, Cancer, Leo, Virgo, Libra, Scorpio, Sagittarius, Capricorn, Aquarius, and Pisces. Each sign is associated with specific elements, qualities, ruling planets, and modalities that further define their unique characteristics. For example, Aries is a fire sign known for its boldness and leadership qualities, while Taurus is an earth sign associated with stability and practicality.

The Zodiac Wheel is divided into four elements: Fire, Earth, Air, and Water. Each element is associated with three zodiac signs, reflecting their shared characteristics and energies. Fire signs (Aries, Leo, Sagittarius) are known for their passion, creativity, and drive. Earth signs (Taurus, Virgo, Capricorn) are grounded, practical, and reliable. Air signs (Gemini, Libra, Aquarius) are intellectual, communicative, and social. Water signs (Cancer, Scorpio, Pisces) are intuitive, emotional, and sensitive.

In addition to the elements, the Zodiac Wheel also includes the modalities: Cardinal, Fixed, and Mutable signs. Cardinal signs (Aries, Cancer, Libra, Capricorn) are initiators and leaders, known for their ambition and drive. Fixed signs (Taurus, Leo, Scorpio, Aquarius) are stable and determined, with a strong sense of purpose. Mutable signs (Gemini, Virgo, Sagittarius, Pisces) are adaptable and flexible, able to navigate change with ease.

Overall, the Zodiac Wheel and its significance in astrology provide a framework for understanding the diverse and complex nature of human personalities. By studying the Zodiac Wheel, individuals can gain insight into their own strengths, weaknesses, and potential for growth. The Zodiac Wheel serves as a valuable tool for self-reflection, personal development, and navigating life's challenges and opportunities based on the cosmic energies at play in the universe.

The Four Elements: Fire, Earth, Air, and Water

The concept of the four elements in astrology – Fire, Earth, Air, and Water – is a fundamental aspect of understanding the zodiac signs and their characteristics. Each element represents a different set of traits, energies, and qualities that influence the personalities of individuals born under corresponding zodiac signs.

Fire Signs (Aries, Leo, Sagittarius):
The Fire signs are known for their passionate and dynamic nature. They are driven by creativity, enthusiasm, and a strong sense of purpose. Fire signs are often seen as bold, assertive, and adventurous. They thrive on taking risks, pursuing their goals with vigor and determination. However, they can also be impulsive, prone to sudden bursts of energy, and sometimes struggle with patience and temperance.

Earth Signs (Taurus, Virgo, Capricorn):
The Earth signs are grounded, practical, and reliable. They are known for their stability, patience, and hard work ethic. Earth signs are deeply connected to the physical world and value security, material possessions, and tangible achievements. They are pragmatic, detail-oriented, and excel in tasks that require organization and structure. While Earth signs can be dependable and loyal, they may also struggle with adaptability and spontaneity.

Air Signs (Gemini, Libra, Aquarius):
The Air signs are intellectual, communicative, and social. They are characterized by their curiosity, wit, and analytical skills. Air signs excel in areas that involve mental agility, problem-solving, and creative expression. They are adept at communication, often engaging in lively debates and discussions. Air signs value freedom, independence, and innovation. However, they may also be prone to indecisiveness, inconsistency, and detachment from emotional matters.

Water Signs (Cancer, Scorpio, Pisces):
The Water signs are sensitive, intuitive, and emotional. They are deeply attuned to their feelings and the emotional undercurrents of the world around them. Water signs are empathetic, compassionate, and nurturing. They excel

in areas that require empathy, intuition, and creativity. Water signs are known for their depth of emotion, empathy, and psychic abilities. However, they may also struggle with boundaries, emotional vulnerability, and mood swings.

Each element plays a crucial role in shaping the personality traits, tendencies, and behaviors of individuals born under specific zodiac signs. Understanding the elemental influences can provide valuable insights into how individuals interact with the world, approach challenges, and navigate relationships. By recognizing and embracing the qualities associated with their elemental sign, individuals can harness their strengths, address their weaknesses, and achieve personal growth and fulfillment in alignment with their astrological nature.

The Modalities: Cardinal, Fixed, and Mutable Signs

In astrology, the zodiac signs are classified into three modalities: Cardinal, Fixed, and Mutable. These modalities play a significant role in understanding the characteristics and behaviors of each sign, as well as how they interact with others. Let's delve deeper into each modality:

1. Cardinal Signs:
The Cardinal signs include Aries, Cancer, Libra, and Capricorn. These signs mark the beginning of each season: Aries for spring, Cancer for summer, Libra for fall, and Capricorn for winter. Cardinal signs are known for their initiative, leadership qualities, and ability to start new projects. They are proactive, ambitious, and eager to take charge. Individuals born under Cardinal signs are often seen as trendsetters and initiators, always ready to take the first step towards achieving their goals. However, they may also be prone to impatience and restlessness if things do not progress as quickly as they would like.

2. Fixed Signs:
The Fixed signs include Taurus, Leo, Scorpio, and Aquarius. These signs fall in the middle of each season, representing stability, determination, and perseverance. Fixed signs are known for their strong willpower, reliability, and resistance to change. Individuals born under Fixed signs are often steadfast in their beliefs and values, making them dependable and loyal friends and partners. They are also known for their determination to see things through to the end, even in the face of challenges. However, Fixed signs may also be prone to stubbornness and rigidity, as they can be resistant to adapting to new circumstances.

3. Mutable Signs:

The Mutable signs include Gemini, Virgo, Sagittarius, and Pisces. These signs mark the end of each season, representing flexibility, adaptability, and change. Mutable signs are known for their versatility, resourcefulness, and ability to go with the flow. Individuals born under Mutable signs are often adept at adjusting to different situations and environments, making them excellent problem solvers and communicators. They are open-minded and curious, always seeking new experiences and knowledge. However, Mutable signs may also be prone to indecisiveness and inconsistency, as they can struggle with making firm decisions or sticking to one path.

Understanding the modalities of Cardinal, Fixed, and Mutable signs can provide valuable insights into how each zodiac sign approaches life, relationships, and challenges. By recognizing these modalities in yourself and others, you can better navigate interpersonal dynamics, leverage your strengths, and work on areas for growth and development. Embracing the diverse qualities of each modality can lead to a more holistic understanding of astrology and a deeper connection to the intricacies of the zodiac.

Chapter 2

Aries

Aries Overview and Symbolism

Aries, the first sign of the zodiac, is symbolized by the Ram, representing courage, leadership, and determination. Individuals born under the sign of Aries are known for their bold and energetic nature, always eager to take on new challenges and lead the way.

Aries is ruled by the planet Mars, the god of war, which contributes to the sign's assertive and competitive qualities. Mars infuses Aries with a fiery energy and a strong desire for action and achievement. Those born under this sign are often driven by a need to succeed and excel in all that they do.

The element associated with Aries is Fire, symbolizing passion, creativity, and inspiration. Aries individuals are known for their fiery personalities, enthusiasm, and zest for life. They are often trailblazers and pioneers, unafraid to venture into uncharted territory and take risks to achieve their goals.

Aries is a Cardinal sign, indicating a strong sense of initiative and leadership. People born under this sign are natural go-getters who are not afraid to take charge and make things happen. They are independent and self-reliant, with a strong sense of determination and self-assurance.

In terms of personality traits, Aries individuals are known for being confident, ambitious, and dynamic. They possess a natural charisma and magnetism that draws others to them. Aries are often described as bold and courageous, always willing to stand up for what they believe in and fight for their convictions.

In love and relationships, Aries is passionate and intense. They are ardent lovers who seek excitement and adventure in their romantic pursuits. Aries individuals are known for their loyalty and devotion to their partners, but they also require a sense of freedom and independence in their relationships.

When it comes to career and ambitions, Aries individuals excel in roles that allow them to showcase their leadership skills and take on new challenges. They thrive in competitive environments and are driven by a desire to achieve success and recognition. Aries are natural entrepreneurs and innovators, always looking for ways to push boundaries and make a mark in their chosen field.

Strengths of Aries include their courage, determination, and resilience. They are natural born leaders who inspire and motivate others with their infectious energy and enthusiasm. Aries are also known for their honesty and straightforwardness, never shying away from speaking their mind or standing up for what they believe in.

However, Aries individuals can also have weaknesses such as impatience, impulsiveness, and a tendency towards being overly competitive. They may sometimes act before thinking things through or come across as overly aggressive in their pursuit of success.

In terms of compatibility with other signs, Aries is most compatible with Leo, Sagittarius, and Aquarius, as they share a similar passion for adventure and excitement. They may find challenges in relationships with Cancer and Capricorn, who have different approaches to emotions and stability.

Famous Aries personalities include renowned figures such as Leonardo da Vinci, Lady Gaga, Mariah Carey, and Elton John, who embody the pioneering spirit and dynamic energy of this sign.

In conclusion, Aries individuals are dynamic, ambitious, and courageous individuals who thrive on challenge and adventure. They are natural leaders and innovators who have the drive and determination to achieve great success in all aspects of their lives.

Personality Traits of Aries

Aries, the first sign of the zodiac, is known for its pioneering spirit and fiery energy. Individuals born under the sign of Aries, which spans from March 21 to April 19, are often seen as natural leaders with a strong sense of independence and determination.

One of the key personality traits of Aries is their boldness and courage. Aries individuals are not afraid to take risks and pursue their goals with unwavering confidence. They are adventurous and thrive in situations that challenge them to push their limits and explore new territories.

Aries individuals are also known for their competitive nature. They have a strong desire to succeed and be the best at whatever they do. This drive for excellence often propels them to achieve great things in both their personal and professional lives.

Furthermore, Aries individuals are highly energetic and enthusiastic. They approach life with a sense of optimism and excitement, always ready to dive headfirst into new experiences and opportunities. Their enthusiasm is infectious and can inspire those around them to take action and follow their lead.

On the flip side, Aries individuals can sometimes be seen as impulsive and impatient. Their quick temper and tendency to act before thinking things through can lead to conflicts and misunderstandings. However, their impulsiveness is often balanced by their ability to bounce back quickly from setbacks and learn from their mistakes.

In relationships, Aries individuals are passionate and devoted partners. They are fiercely loyal and protective of their loved ones, willing to go to great lengths to ensure their happiness and well-being. Aries individuals value honesty and direct communication in their relationships, preferring to address issues head-on rather than letting them fester.

In terms of career and ambitions, Aries individuals excel in roles that allow them to take charge and lead others. They thrive in dynamic and fast-paced environments where they can showcase their initiative and drive. Aries individuals are natural problem-solvers and excel in roles that require quick thinking and decisive action.

Strengths of Aries individuals include their confidence, independence, and resilience. They are natural-born leaders who are not afraid to take the lead and make tough decisions when necessary. Aries individuals are also known for their optimism and enthusiasm, which can inspire others to follow their lead.

On the other hand, Aries individuals may struggle with patience and impulsiveness. They can be quick to anger and may need to work on managing their emotions and reactions in challenging situations. Additionally, Aries individuals may benefit from learning to listen to others and consider different perspectives before making decisions.

In conclusion, Aries individuals are dynamic and driven individuals who bring a sense of energy and excitement to everything they do. Their passion, courage, and determination make them natural leaders and trailblazers who are always ready to take on new challenges and conquer new heights.

Aries in Love and Relationships

Aries, the first sign of the zodiac, is known for their fiery and passionate nature when it comes to love and relationships. People born under the sign of Aries are often described as bold, adventurous, and full of energy, which can make them exciting partners to be with. In this chapter, we will delve deeper into the characteristics, behaviors, and compatibility of Aries in love and relationships.

Personality Traits of Aries in Love:
Aries individuals are known for their enthusiasm and spontaneity, which reflects in their approach to love. They are not afraid to take the lead and make the first move in a relationship. Aries are passionate and intense lovers who enjoy the thrill of the chase and the excitement of new beginnings. However, they can also be impulsive and impatient at times, which may lead to conflicts in relationships.

Aries in Love and Relationships:
In a romantic relationship, Aries is devoted and loyal to their partner. They are fiercely protective of their loved ones and will go to great lengths to ensure their happiness and well-being. Aries individuals value honesty and direct communication in relationships, as they appreciate openness and transparency with their partners. They seek a partner who can match their energy and enthusiasm, someone who can keep up with their adventurous spirit.

Career and Ambitions of Aries:
Aries individuals are ambitious and goal-oriented, which can sometimes make them prioritize their career over their relationships. They are natural leaders

who thrive in competitive environments and enjoy taking on new challenges. In relationships, Aries may need a partner who understands and supports their career aspirations, while also providing emotional support and stability.

Strengths and Weaknesses of Aries in Relationships:
Aries' strengths in relationships lie in their passion, loyalty, and adventurous spirit. They are generous and caring partners who will always be there for their loved ones. However, Aries' weaknesses can include a tendency towards impatience, impulsiveness, and a need for constant excitement and stimulation. Aries individuals may need to work on being more patient and understanding in relationships to ensure long-term success.

Aries Compatibility with Other Signs:
Aries is most compatible with fellow fire signs like Leo and Sagittarius, as they share a similar energy and passion for life. They can also have a strong connection with air signs like Gemini and Aquarius, who can stimulate their intellect and creativity. However, Aries may face challenges in relationships with water signs like Cancer and Pisces, as their emotional depth and sensitivity may clash with Aries' more assertive nature.

Famous Aries Personalities:
Some famous Aries individuals known for their dynamic personalities and leadership qualities include Lady Gaga, Mariah Carey, Robert Downey Jr., and Emma Watson.

In conclusion, Aries individuals bring excitement, passion, and a sense of adventure to their relationships. Their fiery nature and bold demeanor make them captivating partners, but they may need to work on balancing their impulsive tendencies with patience and understanding to foster healthy and fulfilling relationships.

Career and Ambitions of Aries

Aries individuals are known for their bold and fearless nature, often seen as pioneers and leaders in various aspects of life. In terms of career and ambitions, Aries individuals are driven by a strong sense of purpose and a desire to excel in whatever they choose to pursue.

Career paths that align with the natural tendencies of Aries include roles that allow them to take charge and lead others. Aries individuals thrive in dynamic environments that require quick decision-making and a high level of energy. They are natural-born leaders who are not afraid to take risks and push boundaries to achieve their goals.

Ambition runs deep in the Aries personality, as they are constantly seeking new challenges and opportunities for growth. They are not content with mediocrity and strive for excellence in everything they do. Aries individuals are highly competitive and driven to succeed, often setting ambitious goals for themselves and working tirelessly to achieve them.

In the workplace, Aries individuals are known for their strong work ethic and determination. They are not afraid to roll up their sleeves and put in the hard work required to reach their objectives. Aries individuals excel in roles that require independence, initiative, and a proactive approach to problem-solving.

When it comes to career advancement, Aries individuals are not afraid to take the initiative and pursue opportunities for growth and development. They are natural go-getters who are not satisfied with staying stagnant in their careers. Aries individuals are always looking for ways to challenge themselves and push their limits to achieve greater success.

In terms of ambitions, Aries individuals are often driven by a desire to make a significant impact in their chosen field. They have a strong sense of purpose and are motivated by the idea of leaving a lasting legacy through their work. Aries individuals are not content with simply going through the motions – they want to make a real difference and be recognized for their contributions.

Overall, the career and ambitions of Aries individuals are characterized by their drive, determination, and passion for success. They are natural-born leaders who excel in roles that allow them to take charge and make a meaningful impact. With their strong work ethic and competitive spirit, Aries individuals are well-equipped to achieve their goals and reach new heights of success in their chosen careers.

Strengths and Weaknesses of Aries

Aries, the first sign of the zodiac, is known for its bold and courageous nature. Individuals born under the sign of Aries are often seen as pioneers and leaders who are not afraid to take risks and blaze new trails. Understanding the strengths and weaknesses of Aries can provide valuable insights into their personality and behavior.

Strengths of Aries:

1. Leadership Qualities: Aries individuals are natural-born leaders who possess strong leadership qualities. They are decisive, assertive, and confident in their abilities to lead others.

2. Courageous and Adventurous: Aries are known for their courage and adventurous spirit. They are not afraid to take risks and explore new opportunities, making them trailblazers in various aspects of life.

3. Independent and Self-Reliant: Aries value their independence and autonomy. They are self-reliant individuals who prefer to take charge of their own destiny and make decisions based on their own judgment.

4. Energetic and Enthusiastic: Aries are full of energy and enthusiasm, which fuels their drive to pursue their goals and ambitions with passion and vigor.

5. Competitive Nature: Aries thrive in competitive environments and enjoy challenges that push them to excel and achieve success. They have a strong desire to win and come out on top in any situation.

Weaknesses of Aries:

1. Impulsive and Impatient: Aries can be impulsive and impatient at times, leading them to make hasty decisions without considering the consequences. Their impulsive nature can sometimes result in conflicts or misunderstandings.

2. Stubborn and Headstrong: Aries individuals can be stubborn and headstrong, unwilling to compromise or consider alternative perspectives. This can lead to difficulties in relationships and conflicts with others.

3. Short-Tempered: Aries have a tendency to have a quick temper and can become easily agitated or frustrated when things do not go their way. It is important for Aries to work on managing their anger and practicing patience.

4. Reckless Behavior: Due to their adventurous nature, Aries may engage in reckless behavior or take unnecessary risks without fully considering the consequences. It is essential for Aries to exercise caution and think things through before acting impulsively.

5. Competitive to a Fault: While the competitive nature of Aries can drive them to achieve great success, it can also lead to excessive competitiveness and a lack of empathy towards others. Aries should be mindful of balancing their competitive spirit with compassion and understanding.

In conclusion, Aries individuals possess a unique blend of strengths and weaknesses that shape their personality and behavior. By understanding these traits, Aries can leverage their strengths to achieve their goals while working on overcoming their weaknesses for personal growth and development.

Aries Compatibility with Other Signs

Aries, known as the first sign of the zodiac, is represented by the ram and is associated with qualities such as leadership, courage, and dynamism. Individuals born under the Aries sign are known for their adventurous spirit and independent nature. When it comes to compatibility with other signs, Aries has unique dynamics with each astrological sign due to its fiery and assertive nature.

Aries and Taurus: Aries and Taurus have contrasting personalities which can create both harmony and conflict in their relationship. Aries is impulsive and quick to act, while Taurus is grounded and practical. Aries may find Taurus too slow-paced, while Taurus may see Aries as reckless. However, if they can find a balance between Aries' spontaneity and Taurus' stability, they can create a strong and enduring partnership.

Aries and Gemini: Aries and Gemini share a love for excitement and new experiences, making them a dynamic duo. Both signs are energetic and love to socialize, which can lead to a stimulating and lively relationship. Communication is key in this pairing, as Gemini's quick wit and Aries' directness can lead to engaging conversations and a deep emotional connection.

Aries and Cancer: Aries and Cancer have contrasting emotional needs, which can lead to challenges in their relationship. Aries is independent and assertive, while Cancer is nurturing and sensitive. Aries may find Cancer too clingy, while Cancer may feel overwhelmed by Aries' need for independence. However, if they can learn to appreciate and respect each other's differences, they can create a harmonious and fulfilling partnership.

Aries and Leo: Aries and Leo are both fire signs, which means they share a passion for life and a desire for excitement. This combination can lead to a fiery and passionate relationship, with both signs supporting and encouraging each other's ambitions. Aries' boldness complements Leo's confidence, creating a power couple who can achieve great things together.

Aries and Virgo: Aries and Virgo have different approaches to life, which can lead to misunderstandings in their relationship. Aries is spontaneous and adventurous, while Virgo is practical and detail-oriented. Aries may find Virgo too critical, while Virgo may see Aries as reckless. However, if they can find common ground and appreciate each other's strengths, they can create a balanced and harmonious partnership.

Aries and Libra: Aries and Libra have a natural affinity for each other, as both signs value harmony and balance in their relationships. Aries' assertiveness is complemented by Libra's diplomacy, creating a partnership based on mutual respect and understanding. Aries can learn patience and compromise from Libra, while Libra can benefit from Aries' boldness and decisiveness.

Aries and Scorpio: Aries and Scorpio share a deep emotional intensity, which can lead to a passionate and transformative relationship. Both signs are fiercely independent and determined, which can create a strong bond built on trust and loyalty. Aries' assertiveness can sometimes clash with Scorpio's need for control, but if they can find a balance between power dynamics, they can create a profound and fulfilling connection.

Aries and Sagittarius: Aries and Sagittarius are both adventurous and free-spirited signs, making them an ideal match for each other. Both signs value independence and enjoy exploring new horizons, which can lead to a dynamic and exciting relationship. Aries' passion is complemented by Sagittarius' optimism, creating a partnership filled with laughter, adventure, and mutual respect.

In conclusion, Aries' compatibility with other signs varies depending on the unique dynamics and personalities of each pairing. While challenges may arise due to differences in temperament and communication styles, Aries can form strong and fulfilling relationships with signs that complement their fiery and adventurous nature. By understanding and appreciating the strengths and weaknesses of each sign, Aries can navigate the complexities of relationships and find harmony and happiness with their compatible partners.

Famous Aries Personalities

Aries, the first sign of the zodiac, is known for its bold and pioneering spirit. Individuals born under this sign are often dynamic, energetic, and passionate. Many famous personalities across various fields exhibit the typical traits associated with Aries. Let's delve into some of the most notable Aries individuals who have made a mark on the world.

One of the most iconic Aries personalities is Vincent van Gogh, the Dutch post-impressionist painter. Known for his emotionally charged artworks and vivid use of color, van Gogh's creative genius and passionate nature are classic Aries traits. Despite facing personal struggles and mental health issues, van Gogh's artistic legacy continues to inspire people around the globe.

Another prominent Aries figure is Lady Gaga, the American singer, songwriter, and actress. Known for her bold and avant-garde style, Gaga embodies the fearless and independent spirit of Aries. Her boundary-pushing music and performances have earned her critical acclaim and a dedicated fan base. Aries individuals like Lady Gaga are not afraid to be themselves and stand out from the crowd.

In the realm of sports, Aries personalities are often known for their competitive drive and determination. One such figure is legendary tennis player Serena Williams. With her fiery on-court demeanor and exceptional skills, Williams has dominated the tennis world for years. Her relentless pursuit of excellence and unwavering self-belief are quintessential Aries qualities that have propelled her to greatness.

Moving into the world of entertainment, another famous Aries personality is Mariah Carey, the powerhouse vocalist and songwriter. Known for her impressive vocal range and chart-topping hits, Carey's success in the music industry is a testament to her Aries traits of passion and ambition. Her strong-willed nature and unwavering dedication to her craft have solidified her status as a music icon.

In the field of literature, Aries individuals have also left their mark. One such luminary is Maya Angelou, the acclaimed American poet, memoirist, and civil rights activist. Angelou's powerful words and profound insights into the human experience have touched the hearts of readers worldwide. Her courage, resilience, and unwavering commitment to social justice embody the best qualities of Aries.

These are just a few examples of the many famous Aries personalities who have made significant contributions to their respective fields. From art to music, sports to literature, Aries individuals are known for their passion, creativity, and determination. Their fearless pursuit of their goals and unapologetic authenticity serve as inspiration for us all to embrace our unique strengths and forge our own paths to success.

Chapter 3

Taurus

Taurus Overview and Symbolism

Taurus, the second sign of the zodiac, is symbolized by the bull, representing strength, determination, and groundedness. Those born under the sign of Taurus are known for their reliability, practicality, and love for the finer things in life. People born between April 20th and May 20th fall under the Taurus sign, which is ruled by the planet Venus, the planet of love, beauty, and abundance.

The symbol of the bull embodies the Taurus personality traits of persistence, stability, and resilience. Taurus individuals are often described as dependable and loyal, with a strong sense of determination to achieve their goals. They are known for their practical approach to life and their ability to stay grounded even in the face of challenges.

Taurus is an earth sign, along with Virgo and Capricorn, which further emphasizes their grounded nature and connection to the physical world. Earth signs are practical, reliable, and focused on material security and stability. Taurus individuals value comfort and luxury, enjoying the pleasures of life such as good food, beautiful surroundings, and sensual experiences.

In terms of personality traits, Taurus individuals are known for being patient, reliable, and hardworking. They are often described as down-to-earth and practical, with a strong sense of determination and perseverance. Taurus people are also known for their loyalty and commitment to their relationships, making them reliable and trustworthy friends and partners.

In love and relationships, Taurus individuals are affectionate and devoted partners. They value stability and security in their relationships and are willing to put in the effort to make things work. Taurus individuals are known for their romantic nature and their appreciation of the finer things in life, making them attentive and generous partners.

In terms of career and ambitions, Taurus individuals are hardworking and focused on achieving their goals. They excel in roles that require patience, determination, and attention to detail. Taurus individuals are often drawn to careers in fields such as finance, real estate, hospitality, and the arts, where they can use their practical skills and love for beauty to succeed.

Strengths of Taurus individuals include their reliability, loyalty, and determination. They are practical and grounded, with a strong work ethic and a commitment to achieving their goals. Taurus individuals are also known for their patience and persistence, which helps them overcome obstacles and achieve success.

Weaknesses of Taurus individuals include their stubbornness and resistance to change. Taurus individuals can be resistant to new ideas and may struggle to adapt to new situations. They can also be possessive and materialistic at times, valuing material possessions and comfort over other aspects of life.

In terms of compatibility with other signs, Taurus individuals are most compatible with water signs like Cancer and Pisces, as well as earth signs like Virgo and Capricorn. These signs share Taurus's practical nature and appreciation for stability and security, creating harmonious relationships based on mutual understanding and support.

Famous Taurus personalities include actors Dwayne "The Rock" Johnson and Audrey Hepburn, singer Adele, and entrepreneur Mark Zuckerberg. These individuals exemplify the Taurus traits of determination, practicality, and success in their respective fields.

Overall, Taurus individuals are known for their grounded nature, practicality, and determination. They value stability, security, and the finer things in life, making them reliable and loyal friends, partners, and colleagues. Taurus individuals excel in careers that require patience, hard work, and attention to detail, and they have the potential to achieve great success through their perseverance and commitment.

Personality Traits of Taurus

Taurus, the second sign of the zodiac, is represented by the bull, symbolizing strength, determination, and stability. Individuals born under this sign are known for their steadfast and reliable nature. Here is a detailed exploration of the personality traits of Taurus:

1. Reliable and Trustworthy: Taurus individuals are highly dependable and trustworthy. They are known for their consistency and reliability in both personal and professional relationships. People often turn to Taurus for support and guidance due to their unwavering loyalty.

2. Patient and Persistent: Taurus individuals possess a great deal of patience and persistence. They are willing to put in the hard work and effort required to achieve their goals. Taurus is not easily discouraged by obstacles and setbacks, as they have a strong determination to succeed.

3. Practical and Grounded: Taurus individuals have a practical and down-to-earth approach to life. They are rooted in reality and tend to focus on tangible, material aspects of life. Taurus values stability and security, both in their personal and financial affairs.

4. Sensual and Appreciative of Beauty: Taurus individuals have a deep appreciation for the finer things in life. They are drawn to beauty in all its forms, whether it be art, music, or nature. Taurus enjoys indulging their senses and creating a comfortable and aesthetically pleasing environment.

5. Stubborn and Resistant to Change: One of the challenging traits of Taurus is their stubbornness. Once Taurus has made up their mind about something, it can be difficult to sway them in another direction. They are resistant to change and prefer to stick to familiar routines and habits.

6. Possessive and Materialistic: Taurus individuals can be possessive when it comes to their relationships and belongings. They value security and stability, which can sometimes manifest as possessiveness. Taurus also has a tendency to place importance on material possessions and financial security.

7. Loyal and Devoted: Taurus individuals are fiercely loyal and devoted to their loved ones. They form deep and lasting bonds with their family and friends, and they are willing to go to great lengths to support and protect those they care about.

8. Patient and Gentle in Communication: Taurus individuals are known for their calm and gentle communication style. They are good listeners and offer thoughtful advice when needed. Taurus values harmony in relationships and strives to maintain peaceful interactions with others.

In conclusion, Taurus individuals are characterized by their reliability, patience, practicality, and loyalty. While they may struggle with stubbornness and possessiveness at times, their steadfast nature and commitment to those they care about make them valuable and trustworthy companions in both personal and professional settings.

Taurus in Love and Relationships

Taurus, represented by the symbol of the bull, is ruled by Venus, the planet of love and beauty, which greatly influences their approach to romantic connections.

Taurus individuals are known for their loyalty, dependability, and sensuality in relationships. They value stability and security, making them committed partners who seek long-term, meaningful connections. In love, Taurus is patient and steadfast, building a strong foundation based on trust and mutual respect.

When it comes to romance, Taurus is a true romantic at heart. They appreciate gestures of love and affection, such as thoughtful gifts, romantic dinners, and quality time spent together. Taurus individuals are known for their sensual nature, enjoying physical expressions of love and intimacy that deepen their emotional bond with their partner.

In relationships, Taurus can be possessive at times due to their desire for security and stability. They value loyalty and expect the same level of commitment from their partner. Taurus individuals are known to be reliable and dependable, always there for their loved ones through thick and thin.

Communication is key in relationships with Taurus. They appreciate honesty and open communication, as they value trust and transparency in their connections. Taurus individuals are great listeners and offer practical advice and support to their partners when needed.

Taurus individuals are also known for their strong work ethic and determination, which carries over into their relationships. They are willing to put in the effort and hard work to make their relationships thrive and grow over time. Taurus partners are reliable and supportive, always there to lend a helping hand and provide emotional stability.

In terms of compatibility, Taurus individuals are most compatible with water signs like Cancer, Scorpio, and Pisces, as they complement each other's emotional needs and offer a sense of security and understanding in the relationship. Taurus also gets along well with earth signs like Virgo and Capricorn, as they share similar values and priorities in life.

Overall, Taurus individuals approach love and relationships with a grounded and practical mindset, seeking stability, loyalty, and emotional connection in their romantic endeavors. With their nurturing and affectionate nature, Taurus partners create harmonious and lasting relationships built on trust, love, and mutual respect.

Career and Ambitions of Taurus

Taurus is the second sign of the zodiac and is represented by the symbol of the Bull. Individuals born under the Taurus sign are known for their strong and reliable nature, as well as their practical approach to life. In terms of career and ambitions, Taurus individuals are driven by a desire for stability, security, and material success.

Career: Taurus individuals are hardworking and dedicated, making them well-suited for careers that require patience, perseverance, and attention to detail. They excel in roles that involve working with their hands, such as in the fields of agriculture, horticulture, or craftsmanship. Taurus individuals also thrive in positions that allow them to use their practical skills and sense of responsibility, such as in finance, banking, or real estate.

Ambitions: Taurus individuals are ambitious and goal-oriented, with a strong desire to achieve success and financial security. They are not afraid to put in the hard work and effort required to reach their goals, and they are willing to take the necessary steps to secure their future. Taurus individuals are also known for their determination and persistence, which helps them overcome obstacles and challenges along the way.

Taurus individuals value stability and security in their careers, and they are likely to seek out positions that offer job security, a steady income, and opportunities for growth and advancement. They are also drawn to professions that allow them to build something tangible or long-lasting, such as in architecture, construction, or engineering.

Strengths: Taurus individuals are known for their practicality, reliability, and determination. They have a strong work ethic and are willing to put in the effort required to achieve their goals. Taurus individuals are also patient and methodical, which helps them excel in tasks that require attention to detail and precision. Their grounded and down-to-earth nature makes them valuable team members and reliable colleagues.

Weaknesses: Despite their many strengths, Taurus individuals can sometimes be stubborn and resistant to change. They may struggle to adapt to new situations or embrace innovation, preferring instead to stick to what is familiar and comfortable. Taurus individuals may also be possessive or materialistic at times, placing too much emphasis on material possessions or financial success.

Overall, Taurus individuals are driven by a desire for stability, security, and success in their careers. With their practical skills, determination, and strong work ethic, Taurus individuals are well-equipped to achieve their ambitions and build a solid foundation for their future.

Strengths and Weaknesses of Taurus

Taurus is the second sign of the zodiac, represented by the bull, and is known for its grounded and practical nature. Individuals born under the Taurus sign are often seen as reliable, patient, and hardworking. In this chapter, we will explore the strengths and weaknesses of Taurus, shedding light on the key characteristics that define this earth sign.

Strengths of Taurus:

1. Dependable: Taurus individuals are known for their reliability and consistency. They are trustworthy and can be counted on to fulfill their commitments and responsibilities.
2. Patient: Taurus has a remarkable ability to stay calm and composed even in challenging situations. Their patience allows them to approach problems with a steady and rational mindset.
3. Determined: Once a Taurus sets their mind on a goal, they will work diligently towards achieving it. Their strong sense of determination helps them overcome obstacles and persevere in the face of adversity.

4. Practical: Taurus individuals have a practical approach to life. They are grounded in reality and excel at making sound decisions based on practical considerations.

5. Loyal: Loyalty is a cornerstone of Taurus' personality. They value their relationships and are fiercely loyal to their loved ones, standing by them through thick and thin.

Weaknesses of Taurus:

1. Stubborn: Taurus can be extremely stubborn and resistant to change. Their fixed nature can make it challenging for them to adapt to new circumstances or consider alternative perspectives.

2. Materialistic: Taurus has a strong appreciation for the finer things in life, which can sometimes lead to materialistic tendencies. They may prioritize material comfort and possessions over other aspects of life.

3. Possessive: Taurus individuals can be possessive and clingy in relationships. They value security and stability, which can sometimes manifest as possessiveness towards their partners or loved ones.

4. Indulgent: Taurus enjoys indulging in life's pleasures, whether it be food, luxury items, or relaxation. However, this indulgence can sometimes lead to overeating, overspending, or laziness.

5. Resistant to Change: Taurus is resistant to change and may struggle with adapting to new situations or embracing innovation. Their preference for routine and familiarity can hinder their growth and development.

In conclusion, Taurus individuals possess a unique blend of strengths and weaknesses that shape their personality and behavior. By understanding these traits, Taurus individuals can leverage their strengths to achieve their goals while working on overcoming their weaknesses to lead a more balanced and fulfilling life.

Taurus Compatibility with Other Signs

Taurus, the second sign of the zodiac, is known for its stability, practicality, and determination. Individuals born under the Taurus sign are grounded and reliable, seeking security and comfort in all aspects of their lives. When it comes to relationships and compatibility with other zodiac signs, Taurus exhibits unique dynamics that are worth exploring.

Taurus Compatibility with Aries:
Taurus and Aries are neighboring signs in the zodiac, creating a mix of both challenges and opportunities in their relationship. Aries is fiery and impulsive, while Taurus is more grounded and steady. Taurus can provide stability and security to Aries, while Aries can infuse excitement and passion into Taurus' life. Communication and compromise are key for these two signs to find harmony and balance in their relationship.

Taurus Compatibility with Gemini:
Taurus and Gemini have different approaches to life, with Taurus valuing stability and routine, while Gemini seeks variety and intellectual stimulation. Taurus may find Gemini's unpredictability challenging, while Gemini may feel restricted by Taurus' need for security. However, if both partners are willing to appreciate and learn from each other's differences, they can create a dynamic and fulfilling relationship.

Taurus Compatibility with Cancer:
Taurus and Cancer share a deep emotional connection and a strong sense of loyalty and commitment. Both signs value security and home life, creating a harmonious and nurturing bond. Taurus provides stability and practicality, while Cancer offers emotional support and sensitivity. Together, they can build a loving and supportive partnership based on mutual understanding and respect.

Taurus Compatibility with Leo:
Taurus and Leo have contrasting personalities, with Taurus being more introverted and practical, while Leo is outgoing and expressive. Despite their differences, these signs can complement each other well in a relationship. Taurus admires Leo's confidence and charisma, while Leo appreciates Taurus' loyalty and reliability. It is essential for both partners to communicate openly and respect each other's needs to maintain a healthy and balanced relationship.

Taurus Compatibility with Virgo:
Taurus and Virgo share a similar practical and analytical approach to life, making them a highly compatible match. Both signs value stability, hard work, and attention to detail, creating a strong foundation for their relationship. Taurus appreciates Virgo's intelligence and organization, while Virgo admires

Taurus' determination and reliability. Together, they can build a harmonious and supportive partnership based on mutual respect and shared values.

In conclusion, Taurus compatibility with other signs varies based on the unique dynamics and interactions between each pair. By understanding and appreciating the strengths and weaknesses of each sign, individuals can navigate relationships more effectively and build stronger connections based on mutual understanding and respect.

Famous Taurus Personalities

Taurus, the second sign of the zodiac, is known for its steadfast and reliable nature. People born under this earth sign, which is ruled by Venus, are often characterized by their practicality, determination, and love for stability. Famous Taurus personalities exhibit these traits in various aspects of their lives, making them stand out in their respective fields.

One of the most famous Taurus personalities is Audrey Hepburn, born on May 4, 1929. This iconic actress and humanitarian embodied the grace and elegance commonly associated with Taurus individuals. Known for her timeless beauty and talent, Hepburn captivated audiences with her performances in classic films such as "Breakfast at Tiffany's" and "Roman Holiday." Beyond her acting career, Hepburn also dedicated herself to humanitarian work as a UNICEF Goodwill Ambassador, showcasing the Taurus traits of generosity and compassion.

Another notable Taurus personality is Dwayne "The Rock" Johnson, born on May 2, 1972. This successful actor, producer, and former professional wrestler exemplifies the Taurus traits of determination and hard work. Johnson's rise to fame from his wrestling days to becoming one of Hollywood's highest-paid actors showcases his unwavering dedication to his craft. His strong work ethic and resilience have earned him a reputation as a versatile performer and a role model for many.

Additionally, Taurus individuals are known for their practicality and down-to-earth nature, traits exemplified by Mark Zuckerberg, born on May 14, 1984. As the co-founder and CEO of Facebook, Zuckerberg revolutionized social media and technology, embodying the Taurus traits of stability and perseverance. His strategic vision and focus on building a sustainable platform for connecting people worldwide reflect the Taurus dedication to creating lasting foundations for success.

Furthermore, Taurus personalities are often admired for their loyalty and reliability, qualities that are evident in the work of Cate Blanchett, born on May 14, 1969. This award-winning actress is known for her versatility and commitment to her craft, showcasing the Taurus traits of consistency and dependability. Blanchett's range of performances in both film and theater has earned her critical acclaim and a reputation as one of the most respected actors in the industry.

In conclusion, famous Taurus personalities embody the core characteristics of this zodiac sign, including determination, practicality, reliability, and loyalty. From the timeless elegance of Audrey Hepburn to the resilience of Dwayne Johnson, Taurus individuals make their mark through their unwavering dedication to their passions and their ability to create lasting impact in their respective fields. These renowned figures serve as inspirations for Taurus individuals and exemplify the strengths and qualities associated with this steadfast and grounded sign.

Chapter 4

Gemini

Gemini Overview and Symbolism

Gemini is the third sign of the zodiac, symbolized by the Twins. This dual symbolism represents the multifaceted nature of Gemini individuals, who are known for their duality, adaptability, and versatility. Ruled by Mercury, the planet of communication and intellect, Geminis are characterized by their sharp minds, curiosity, and love for learning.

Personality Traits of Gemini:

Geminis are known for their quick wit, intelligence, and sociability. They are excellent communicators and have a way with words, making them adept at expressing themselves and connecting with others. Geminis are curious by nature and always seeking new experiences and knowledge. They have a restless energy that drives them to explore different interests and engage in diverse activities.

Gemini in Love and Relationships:

In relationships, Geminis are charming, playful, and affectionate. They value intellectual stimulation and enjoy engaging in lively conversations with their partners. However, Geminis can also be indecisive and struggle with commitment at times, as they may fear being tied down or missing out on other opportunities. It is important for Geminis to find a partner who can keep up with their dynamic nature and provide them with the freedom they crave.

Career and Ambitions of Gemini:

In the professional realm, Geminis excel in careers that allow them to utilize their communication skills and intellectual abilities. They are well-suited for roles that involve writing, public speaking, sales, marketing, and media. Geminis thrive in fast-paced environments that offer variety and intellectual stimulation. They are adaptable and quick learners, making them valuable assets in any workplace.

Strengths and Weaknesses of Gemini:

Some of the key strengths of Geminis include their intelligence, versatility, adaptability, and sociability. They are great problem-solvers, creative thinkers, and adept at multitasking. However, Geminis can also be prone to inconsistency, restlessness, and superficiality. They may struggle with focusing on one thing for too long and can be perceived as flighty or unreliable.

Gemini Compatibility with Other Signs:

Geminis are most compatible with Libra, Aquarius, Aries, and Leo. These signs share Geminis' love for intellectual pursuits, socializing, and adventurous spirit. Geminis may struggle with signs that are more emotionally intense or demanding, such as Scorpio or Capricorn. It is important for Geminis to find partners who can appreciate their need for freedom and mental stimulation.

Famous Gemini Personalities:

Some famous Gemini personalities include Johnny Depp, Angelina Jolie, Kanye West, Marilyn Monroe, and Prince. These individuals exemplify the diverse talents, creativity, and charisma that are often associated with Geminis.

In conclusion, Geminis are known for their intelligence, adaptability, and sociability. Their dual nature and love for communication make them engaging and dynamic individuals who thrive in diverse environments. Geminis bring a unique blend of creativity, curiosity, and wit to everything they do, making them truly one-of-a-kind personalities in the zodiac.

Personality Traits of Gemini

Gemini, the third sign of the zodiac, is represented by the symbol of the Twins, epitomizing duality and versatility. Individuals born under the sign of Gemini are known for their dynamic and adaptable nature. Here is a detailed exploration of the personality traits that define Gemini individuals:

1. Intellectual Curiosity: Geminis are curious beings with a thirst for knowledge. They possess sharp intellects and are constantly seeking to expand their mental horizons. Their inquisitive nature drives them to explore a wide range of subjects and engage in stimulating conversations.

2. Communication Skills: Communication is a forte for Geminis. They are adept at expressing themselves eloquently and engaging others in lively discussions. Their verbal dexterity and wit make them natural conversationalists who can charm and captivate those around them.

3. Versatility and Adaptability: Geminis are known for their ability to adapt to various situations and environments with ease. They are flexible individuals who can navigate change effortlessly, making them versatile in their pursuits and interactions.

4. Social Butterfly: Geminis thrive in social settings and enjoy interacting with diverse groups of people. They have a wide circle of friends and acquaintances due to their sociable and outgoing nature. Their charm and charisma make them magnetic personalities in social gatherings.

5. Restless and Impulsive: Geminis have a restless energy that drives them to seek new experiences and challenges. They can be impulsive at times, craving excitement and variety in their lives. This adventurous spirit fuels their desire for constant stimulation and growth.

6. Dual Nature: The symbol of the Twins reflects the dual nature of Geminis. They can exhibit contrasting traits such as being sociable yet introspective, rational yet emotional. This duality can sometimes lead to inner conflicts but also contributes to their complexity and depth.

7. Playful and Youthful: Geminis have a youthful exuberance and playful spirit that endears them to others. They approach life with a sense of curiosity and a light-hearted attitude, finding joy in the simple pleasures and spontaneity of the moment.

8. Inconsistent and Indecisive: Geminis may struggle with indecision and inconsistency due to their ever-changing interests and perspectives. Their dual nature can lead to wavering opinions and difficulties in committing to long-term goals or relationships.

9. Quick Learners: Geminis possess sharp minds and quick thinking abilities that enable them to grasp new concepts rapidly. They excel in learning diverse skills and adapting to evolving situations, making them versatile and resourceful individuals.

10. Adventurous and Experimental: Geminis are adventurous souls who are willing to take risks and explore uncharted territories. They thrive on novelty and innovation, always seeking new experiences that stimulate their intellect and creativity.

In conclusion, Gemini individuals embody a unique blend of intellectual curiosity, social charm, adaptability, and duality that shape their dynamic personalities. Their versatile nature and insatiable thirst for knowledge make them engaging and multifaceted individuals who constantly seek growth and exploration in all aspects of life.

Gemini in Love and Relationships

Gemini, the third sign of the zodiac, is ruled by the planet Mercury and is known for its dual nature, symbolized by the Twins. Individuals born under the sign of Gemini are known for their charming, witty, and adaptable nature, making them great communicators and social butterflies. When it comes to love and relationships, Geminis bring a unique blend of excitement, intellectual stimulation, and versatility to the table.

In love, Geminis value mental connection and communication above all else. They are drawn to partners who can engage them in stimulating conversations, share their interests, and keep up with their quick-witted banter. Geminis are curious and constantly seeking new experiences, so they thrive in relationships that offer variety and intellectual challenges.

One of the strengths of Geminis in relationships is their adaptability and versatility. They are open-minded and willing to try new things, making them flexible partners who can easily adjust to different situations. Geminis are also known for their playful and fun-loving nature, bringing a sense of lightness and humor to their relationships.

However, Geminis can sometimes struggle with consistency and commitment in relationships. Their dual nature can lead to indecisiveness and restlessness, making it challenging for them to settle down or stay focused on one partner for an extended period. Geminis may also have a tendency to intellectualize their emotions, which can sometimes create a disconnect in their relationships.

In romantic relationships, Geminis are passionate and expressive lovers who enjoy exploring both the physical and emotional aspects of intimacy. They are curious and experimental, always looking for new ways to keep the spark alive in their relationships. Geminis are known for their flirtatious nature and love of playful banter, which can add excitement and energy to their romantic connections.

When it comes to compatibility, Geminis are most compatible with fellow air signs like Libra and Aquarius, as well as fire signs like Aries, Leo, and Sagittarius. These signs share Geminis' love for communication, intellectual stimulation, and adventure, creating a harmonious and dynamic relationship dynamic.

Overall, Geminis bring a unique blend of charm, wit, and versatility to their love and relationships. They thrive on mental connection, communication, and variety, making them engaging and exciting partners for those who can keep up with their fast-paced and ever-evolving nature. By embracing their strengths and working on their challenges, Geminis can create fulfilling and dynamic relationships that keep them intellectually stimulated and emotionally fulfilled.

Career and Ambitions of Gemini

Gemini, the third sign of the zodiac, is known for its dynamic and versatile nature. Individuals born under the sign of Gemini are often characterized by their intelligence, curiosity, and adaptability, making them well-suited for a variety of career paths and ambitions.

1. Versatility: Geminis are known for their versatility and ability to excel in various fields. They are quick learners who can easily adapt to new situations and thrive in environments that require flexibility and multitasking. This versatility allows Geminis to pursue a wide range of career options and explore different interests throughout their professional lives.

2. Communication Skills: Geminis are natural communicators with a gift for expressing ideas and connecting with others. This makes them well-suited for careers in fields such as journalism, public relations, marketing, writing, or sales. Geminis excel in roles that require effective communication, networking, and the ability to convey complex ideas in a clear and engaging manner.

3. Intellectual Curiosity: Geminis have a keen intellect and a thirst for knowledge. They are constantly seeking new information and experiences, making them well-suited for careers in research, education, technology, or any field that requires critical thinking and problem-solving skills. Geminis thrive in environments that stimulate their intellect and allow them to constantly learn and grow.

4. Creativity: Geminis are creative individuals who often have a talent for artistic expression and innovative thinking. They may excel in careers in the arts, design, media, or entertainment industry, where their creativity and originality can shine. Geminis are not afraid to think outside the box and push boundaries, making them valuable assets in creative and innovative fields.

5. Entrepreneurial Spirit: Geminis are natural entrepreneurs who are not afraid to take risks and pursue their ambitions. They have a strong sense of independence and a knack for spotting opportunities. Geminis may thrive in entrepreneurial ventures, startups, or freelance work, where they can leverage their skills, creativity, and adaptability to build successful businesses and projects.

6. Challenges: While Geminis have many strengths that make them well-suited for a variety of careers, they may also face challenges such as indecisiveness, restlessness, and a tendency to get bored easily. It is important for Geminis to find balance in their careers and pursue opportunities that provide mental stimulation, variety, and room for growth and advancement.

In conclusion, Geminis are versatile, creative, and intellectually curious individuals who are well-suited for a wide range of career paths and ambitions. Whether they choose to pursue a career in communication, technology, entrepreneurship, or the arts, Geminis can thrive in roles that allow them to express their creativity, intellect, and adaptability. By embracing their strengths and overcoming challenges, Geminis can achieve success and fulfillment in their professional lives.

Strengths and Weaknesses of Gemini

Gemini, the third sign of the zodiac, is known for its dual nature symbolized by the Twins. People born under the sign of Gemini, typically falling between May 21 and June 20, are often characterized by their versatility, wit, and sociability. In this section, we will delve deeper into the strengths and weaknesses of Gemini individuals.

Strengths of Gemini:

1. Adaptability: Geminis are highly adaptable individuals who can easily navigate through different situations and environments. They are quick to adjust to changes and thrive in diverse settings.

2. Intellectual Curiosity: Known for their sharp intellect and inquisitive nature, Geminis have a thirst for knowledge and are always eager to learn new things. They excel in communication and are skilled at expressing their ideas effectively.

3. Versatility: Geminis possess a diverse range of interests and talents, making them versatile individuals. They can excel in multiple areas and are often seen juggling various projects simultaneously.

4. Charming and Social: With their charismatic personality and excellent communication skills, Geminis are natural social butterflies. They have a way with words and can easily connect with people from all walks of life.

5. Energetic and Agile: Geminis are known for their high energy levels and agility. They are constantly on the move, seeking new experiences and adventures to keep themselves stimulated and engaged.

Weaknesses of Gemini:

1. Indecisiveness: One of the key weaknesses of Geminis is their tendency to be indecisive. Their dual nature can lead to conflicting thoughts and difficulty in making firm decisions.

2. Restlessness: Geminis can easily get bored with routine and crave constant stimulation and excitement. This restlessness can sometimes make it challenging for them to focus on long-term goals.

3. Superficiality: Due to their love for variety and novelty, Geminis may struggle with depth in relationships or tasks. They can sometimes come across as superficial or lacking in commitment.

4. Inconsistency: Geminis can be inconsistent in their actions and emotions, leading to unpredictability in their behavior. This inconsistency can sometimes create confusion for both themselves and those around them.

5. Tendency towards Gossip: Geminis, being excellent communicators, may sometimes fall into the trap of gossip or spreading rumors. Their love for chatter and information can sometimes lead to misunderstandings or conflicts.

In conclusion, Geminis possess a unique blend of strengths and weaknesses that shape their personalities and interactions with the world. By embracing their strengths such as adaptability, curiosity, and versatility, and working on overcoming their weaknesses like indecisiveness and superficiality, Geminis can harness their potential for personal growth and success in various aspects of their lives.

Gemini Compatibility with Other Signs

Gemini, represented by the Twins, is an air sign known for their adaptability, intelligence, and sociable nature. Individuals born under the sign of Gemini are curious, witty, and have a natural ability to communicate effectively. When it comes to relationships, Geminis seek mental stimulation, variety, and freedom. Let's explore how Gemini's characteristics interact with different zodiac signs in terms of compatibility:

1. Aries (March 21 - April 19):
Gemini and Aries share a dynamic and energetic connection. Both signs are independent and enjoy new experiences. Aries admires Gemini's intelligence and wit, while Gemini appreciates Aries' passion and drive. However, conflicts may arise due to Aries' impulsiveness and Gemini's indecisiveness.

2. Taurus (April 20 - May 20):
Gemini and Taurus have contrasting traits that can either complement or clash with each other. Taurus values stability and security, while Gemini seeks change and excitement. Communication may be a challenge as Taurus tends to be more practical and grounded, while Gemini is more abstract and flexible.

3. Cancer (June 21 - July 22):
Gemini and Cancer have different emotional needs and communication styles. Cancer is sensitive and nurturing, while Gemini is more rational and detached.

While Cancer seeks security and stability in relationships, Gemini may find this restrictive. Finding a balance between Cancer's emotional depth and Gemini's intellectual approach is key to a harmonious relationship.

4. Leo (July 23 - August 22):
Gemini and Leo share a love for excitement, creativity, and socializing. Both signs are outgoing and enjoy being the center of attention. Leo's warmth and generosity complement Gemini's charm and wit. However, conflicts may arise due to Leo's need for admiration and Gemini's tendency to flirt or be non-committal.

5. Virgo (August 23 - September 22):
Gemini and Virgo have a natural intellectual rapport and enjoy engaging in stimulating conversations. Virgo appreciates Gemini's versatility and adaptability, while Gemini admires Virgo's attention to detail and practicality. However, Virgo's critical nature and Gemini's scattered energy may lead to misunderstandings if not addressed.

6. Libra (September 23 - October 22):
Gemini and Libra share a harmonious and intellectually stimulating relationship. Both signs value communication, harmony, and social connections. Libra's elegance and charm complement Gemini's wit and versatility. Together, they can create a dynamic and balanced partnership based on mutual understanding and respect.

7. Scorpio (October 23 - November 21):
Gemini and Scorpio have contrasting personalities that can either create intense chemistry or lead to conflicts. Scorpio is passionate, intense, and secretive, while Gemini is light-hearted, curious, and open-minded. Trust and communication are crucial in bridging the gap between Scorpio's depth and Gemini's lightness.

8. Sagittarius (November 22 - December 21):
Gemini and Sagittarius share a natural affinity for adventure, freedom, and intellectual pursuits. Both signs are optimistic, outgoing, and love exploring new ideas and experiences. Sagittarius' philosophical nature complements Gemini's curiosity and wit. Together, they can have a fun and intellectually stimulating relationship filled with laughter and excitement.

In conclusion, Gemini's compatibility with other signs varies based on the unique dynamics between individuals. Communication, mutual respect, and willingness to understand and appreciate each other's differences are key to fostering harmonious relationships for Gemini.

Famous Gemini Personalities

Gemini, the third sign of the zodiac, is represented by the symbol of the Twins. People born under the sign of Gemini, typically falling between May 21 and June 20, are known for their curious and communicative nature. They are versatile individuals who thrive in social settings and possess a quick wit and sharp intellect. Famous Gemini personalities embody these traits and have made significant contributions to various fields. Here are some notable figures who share the Gemini zodiac sign:

1. Marilyn Monroe (June 1, 1926) – An iconic actress and model, Marilyn Monroe captivated audiences with her beauty and talent. Her Gemini charm and charisma made her a beloved figure in Hollywood during the 1950s and 1960s.

2. Angelina Jolie (June 4, 1975) – A versatile actress, filmmaker, and humanitarian, Angelina Jolie is known for her captivating performances on screen and her philanthropic efforts off-screen. Her Gemini versatility and adaptability have allowed her to excel in multiple roles.

3. Johnny Depp (June 9, 1963) – An acclaimed actor known for his diverse roles in films such as "Pirates of the Caribbean" and "Edward Scissorhands," Johnny Depp embodies the Gemini traits of versatility and creativity in his acting career.

4. Kanye West (June 8, 1977) – A multi-talented musician, fashion designer, and entrepreneur, Kanye West is known for pushing boundaries and redefining genres in the music industry. His Gemini energy fuels his innovative approach to art and creativity.

5. Venus Williams (June 17, 1980) – A legendary tennis player and Olympic gold medalist, Venus Williams is known for her athleticism and competitive spirit. Her Gemini adaptability and quick thinking on the court have helped her achieve success in the world of professional sports.

6. Paul McCartney (June 18, 1942) – A music icon and member of the legendary band The Beatles, Paul McCartney is a talented singer-songwriter and instrumentalist. His Gemini versatility and creativity have produced timeless songs that have resonated with audiences for decades.

7. Nicole Kidman (June 20, 1967) – An award-winning actress known for her diverse roles in film and television, Nicole Kidman's Gemini intelligence and adaptability have earned her critical acclaim and accolades in the entertainment industry.

These famous Gemini personalities exemplify the traits commonly associated with this zodiac sign – versatility, creativity, intelligence, and adaptability. Their contributions to various fields showcase the diverse talents and capabilities of individuals born under the sign of Gemini. Whether in the realms of entertainment, sports, music, or philanthropy, these individuals have left a lasting impact on their respective industries and continue to inspire others with their Gemini charm and charisma.

Chapter 5

Cancer

Cancer Overview and Symbolism

Cancer is the fourth sign of the zodiac, represented by the symbol of the Crab. Individuals born between June 21 and July 22 fall under this water sign, known for their nurturing and sensitive nature. Cancer is ruled by the Moon, which influences their emotions and intuition, making them deeply connected to their feelings and those of others.

Symbolism:

The symbol of the Crab represents the protective shell that Cancer individuals often retreat into when feeling vulnerable or threatened. Just like the Crab, they have a hard exterior that shields their soft and sensitive interior. This symbolism highlights Cancer's instinct to protect themselves and their loved ones, as well as their ability to adapt to changing situations with ease.

Personality Traits:

Cancer individuals are known for their caring and empathetic nature. They are highly intuitive and have a strong sense of empathy, making them excellent listeners and sources of emotional support for others. Their nurturing qualities extend to their loved ones, as they are deeply devoted to their families and friends, often putting their needs above their own.

In Love and Relationships:

Cancer individuals are romantic and deeply committed partners. They value emotional intimacy and seek a strong emotional connection in their relationships. Their intuitive nature allows them to understand their partner's feelings without the need for explicit communication. However, they can be prone to mood swings and occasional clinginess due to their sensitive nature.

Career and Ambitions:

In the professional realm, Cancer individuals excel in roles that allow them to utilize their nurturing and empathetic qualities. They thrive in careers where they can provide care and support to others, such as nursing, counseling, or social work. Their strong intuition also makes them adept at roles that require emotional intelligence and understanding.

Strengths and Weaknesses:
Cancer individuals are compassionate, loyal, and deeply intuitive. They possess a strong sense of empathy and are natural caregivers. However, they can be prone to moodiness and clinginess, as well as a tendency to hold onto past hurts. Cancer individuals may struggle with setting boundaries and may become easily overwhelmed by their emotions.

Compatibility with Other Signs:
Cancer individuals are most compatible with other water signs like Scorpio and Pisces, as well as earth signs like Taurus and Virgo. These signs provide the emotional support and stability that Cancer craves in their relationships. However, they may struggle in relationships with fire signs like Aries or Sagittarius, as their emotional needs may not be fully understood.

Famous Cancer Personalities:
Some famous Cancer individuals include Princess Diana, Tom Hanks, Meryl Streep, and Selena Gomez. These individuals exemplify the nurturing and empathetic qualities commonly associated with the Cancer sign.

In conclusion, Cancer individuals are compassionate and intuitive beings who value emotional connections and nurturing relationships. Their protective nature and strong intuition make them valuable assets in both personal and professional settings, where they can provide care and support to those in need.

Personality Traits of Cancer

Cancer, the fourth sign of the zodiac, is represented by the symbol of the crab. People born under the Cancer sign are known for their nurturing and caring nature. They are deeply intuitive and emotional individuals who are guided by their strong connection to their feelings and instincts.

One of the key personality traits of Cancer individuals is their deep sense of empathy and compassion. They are highly attuned to the emotions of those around them and often go out of their way to provide comfort and support to others. Cancerians are natural caregivers and are known for their ability to create a warm and nurturing environment for their loved ones.

Cancerians are also highly protective of their loved ones and place a strong emphasis on family and home life. They are fiercely loyal and dedicated to their relationships, often forming deep and lasting bonds with their partners, friends, and family members. Cancer individuals prioritize their loved ones above all else and will do whatever it takes to ensure their happiness and well-being.

Another defining trait of Cancerians is their strong intuition and sensitivity. They have a keen sense of emotional intelligence and are able to pick up on subtle cues and vibes in their environment. Cancer individuals are deeply in touch with their own emotions and are able to empathize with the feelings of others, making them excellent listeners and confidants.

On the flip side, Cancer individuals can sometimes be prone to moodiness and emotional sensitivity. Their strong emotional nature can lead them to be easily hurt or offended, and they may retreat into their shells when feeling overwhelmed or vulnerable. Cancerians may also have a tendency to hold onto past hurts and grievances, which can sometimes impact their ability to move forward in a positive and constructive manner.

Despite their sensitive nature, Cancerians are also known for their tenacity and determination. Once they set their sights on a goal or objective, they will work tirelessly to achieve it. Cancer individuals are resourceful problem-solvers who are not afraid to roll up their sleeves and put in the hard work necessary to succeed.

In conclusion, Cancer individuals are characterized by their nurturing and empathetic nature, their strong intuition and sensitivity, and their fierce loyalty and dedication to their loved ones. While they may sometimes struggle with emotional vulnerability and moodiness, Cancerians possess a deep well of inner strength and resilience that allows them to overcome obstacles and thrive in all aspects of their lives.

Cancer in Love and Relationships

Cancer is known as the nurturer of the zodiac, and this trait is also reflected in their approach to love and relationships. People born under the sign of Cancer are deeply emotional and sensitive individuals who prioritize creating a sense of security and comfort in their relationships.

Cancerians are known for their loyalty and devotion to their partners. They are highly intuitive and empathetic, making them attuned to the emotional needs of their loved ones. In a romantic relationship, Cancer seeks a deep emotional connection and a sense of intimacy with their partner. They are nurturing and caring, often taking on the role of the caregiver in the relationship.

Cancerians are also known for their protective nature. They value security and stability in their relationships and will go to great lengths to protect their loved ones. They are fiercely loyal and committed, making them reliable partners who can be counted on in times of need.

However, Cancerians can also be quite sensitive and prone to mood swings. They can be easily hurt by perceived slights or rejection, and may retreat into their shell when they feel vulnerable. It's important for their partners to be understanding and patient with Cancer's emotional fluctuations, offering support and reassurance when needed.

In relationships, Cancerians are known for their nurturing and attentive nature. They enjoy creating a warm and cozy home environment, where they can express their love through acts of service and thoughtful gestures. They are romantic at heart and value sentimental gestures that show their partner how much they care.

When it comes to communication in relationships, Cancerians can be quite indirect and may rely on non-verbal cues to express their feelings. They are deeply intuitive and can often pick up on their partner's emotions without the need for words. It's important for their partners to be attentive and sensitive to Cancer's emotional needs, offering them a safe space to express themselves openly and honestly.

In terms of compatibility, Cancerians are most compatible with water signs like Scorpio and Pisces, as well as earth signs like Taurus and Virgo. These signs share Cancer's emotional depth and value intimacy in relationships, creating a strong foundation for a lasting and fulfilling partnership.

Overall, Cancerians bring a deep sense of emotional depth and nurturing energy to their relationships. They are devoted partners who seek a deep emotional connection and a sense of security with their loved ones. By understanding and appreciating Cancer's sensitive and caring nature, their partners can build a strong and loving relationship based on mutual trust and emotional intimacy.

Career and Ambitions of Cancer

Cancer individuals are known for their nurturing and caring nature, which extends beyond their personal relationships into their career and ambitions. Those born under the sign of Cancer are driven by a desire to provide emotional support and create a sense of security for themselves and others. Here is a detailed exploration of the career tendencies and ambitions of Cancer individuals:

Career Traits of Cancer:

Cancer individuals are intuitive and empathetic, making them well-suited for roles that involve caring for others, such as nursing, counseling, social work, or education. Their strong emotional intelligence allows them to connect with people on a deep level, making them excellent listeners and supportive colleagues. Cancerians are also creative and imaginative, which can lead them to pursue careers in the arts, design, or writing.

Ambitions of Cancer:

Cancer individuals are highly ambitious, but their ambitions are often tied to their desire to create a secure and stable environment for themselves and their loved ones. They may strive for financial security, a comfortable home, and a strong support system. Cancerians are family-oriented and often prioritize their relationships and personal life over their career ambitions. However, this does not mean they lack drive or determination. Cancer individuals are dedicated workers who are willing to put in the effort to achieve their goals.

Career Paths for Cancer:

Cancer individuals excel in careers that allow them to use their nurturing and supportive nature. They may find fulfillment in roles that involve caregiving, such as nursing, social work, or childcare. Careers in psychology or counseling also appeal to Cancerians, as they can leverage their emotional intelligence to help others navigate their struggles. Cancer individuals may also thrive in creative fields, such as art, writing, or music, where they can express their emotions and connect with others on a deep level.

Strengths and Weaknesses in Career:
Cancer individuals bring many strengths to the workplace, including empathy, intuition, and creativity. They are highly attuned to the needs of others and excel in roles that require compassion and understanding. However, Cancerians may struggle with setting boundaries and separating their personal and professional lives. Their emotional nature can sometimes lead to mood swings or sensitivity to criticism, which may impact their performance at work. Cancer individuals should work on developing resilience and assertiveness to succeed in their careers.

Overall, Cancer individuals are driven by a desire to care for others and create a sense of security and stability in their lives. Their nurturing and empathetic nature makes them valuable assets in any workplace, particularly in roles that involve supporting and helping others. By leveraging their strengths and addressing their weaknesses, Cancer individuals can achieve success and fulfillment in their careers.

Strengths and Weaknesses of Cancer

Cancer, the fourth sign of the zodiac, is symbolized by the Crab. Those born under the sign of Cancer, typically falling between June 21 and July 22, are known for their nurturing and sensitive nature. In this section, we will delve into the strengths and weaknesses of Cancer individuals.

Strengths of Cancer:

1. Emotional Sensitivity: Cancerians are highly attuned to their own emotions as well as the feelings of those around them. They possess a deep sense of empathy and compassion, making them excellent listeners and caregivers.

2. Loyalty: Cancer individuals are fiercely loyal to their loved ones. They value family and close friendships, and will go to great lengths to protect and support those they care about.

3. Intuitive: Cancerians have a strong intuitive sense that guides them in decision-making and relationships. They are often able to pick up on subtle cues and understand the emotions of others without words being spoken.

4. Creativity: Many Cancer individuals are naturally creative and artistic. They have a vivid imagination and are drawn to activities that allow them to express themselves through art, music, or other forms of creative expression.

5. Tenacity: Despite their sensitive nature, Cancerians possess a strong sense of determination and resilience. They are able to weather life's challenges with grace and perseverance.

Weaknesses of Cancer:

1. Overly Emotional: While their emotional sensitivity is a strength, it can also be a weakness for Cancer individuals. They may be prone to mood swings and emotional outbursts, especially when feeling overwhelmed or insecure.

2. Overprotective: Cancerians have a strong desire to protect their loved ones, sometimes to the point of being overbearing. They may struggle to let go and allow others to make their own choices and mistakes.

3. Clinginess: Cancer individuals value close relationships and may become overly attached to others, seeking constant reassurance and validation. This can put strain on relationships and lead to feelings of suffocation.

4. Indecisiveness: Due to their emotional nature, Cancerians may struggle with making decisions, especially when faced with choices that involve their emotions. They may be prone to second-guessing themselves and seeking external validation.

5. Avoidance of Conflict: Cancer individuals tend to avoid confrontation and conflict, preferring to keep the peace. While this can be a positive trait in some situations, it may also lead to unresolved issues and pent-up emotions.

In conclusion, Cancer individuals possess a unique blend of strengths and weaknesses that shape their personality and interactions with the world. By recognizing and embracing these traits, Cancerians can harness their strengths to nurture relationships and achieve personal growth, while also working to overcome their weaknesses for a more balanced and fulfilling life.

Cancer Compatibility with Other Signs

Cancer, the nurturing and sensitive sign of the zodiac, is known for its emotional depth and strong intuition. In relationships, Cancer seeks security, emotional connection, and a sense of belonging. Understanding Cancer's compatibility with other signs can provide valuable insights into how they interact and relate with different personalities.

1. Cancer and Aries Compatibility:

Cancer and Aries have contrasting personalities that can lead to both challenges and growth in their relationship. Aries is bold, assertive, and independent, while Cancer is more nurturing and emotionally sensitive. Aries may find Cancer's emotional depth comforting, but may also feel suffocated by Cancer's need for security and stability. Cancer may appreciate Aries' confidence and passion, but may struggle with Aries' impulsive nature. Building trust and communication is key for these two signs to navigate their differences and find common ground.

2. Cancer and Taurus Compatibility:

Cancer and Taurus share a deep emotional connection and a love for security and stability. Taurus values loyalty, commitment, and reliability, which align well with Cancer's nurturing nature. Both signs appreciate the comforts of home and value a strong foundation in their relationships. Taurus provides stability and practicality, while Cancer offers emotional support and understanding. Together, they create a harmonious and nurturing partnership built on trust and mutual respect.

3. Cancer and Gemini Compatibility:

Cancer and Gemini have contrasting personalities that can create a dynamic and challenging relationship. Gemini is outgoing, curious, and adaptable, while Cancer is introspective, emotional, and sensitive. Gemini may struggle to understand Cancer's need for emotional security and may find Cancer too clingy or possessive at times. Cancer may feel overwhelmed by Gemini's constant need for variety and stimulation. Open communication and compromise are essential for these two signs to bridge their differences and create a balanced relationship.

4. Cancer and Leo Compatibility:

Cancer and Leo bring different strengths to a relationship, with Cancer's emotional depth complementing Leo's confidence and charisma. Leo is warm, generous, and expressive, while Cancer is nurturing, intuitive, and empathetic. Leo appreciates Cancer's caring nature and emotional support, while Cancer admires Leo's leadership abilities and passion. Both signs value loyalty and commitment in relationships, creating a strong foundation for a lasting and fulfilling partnership. Balancing emotional sensitivity with Leo's need for attention and recognition is key for these two signs to thrive together.

5. Cancer and Virgo Compatibility:

Cancer and Virgo share a strong emotional bond and a desire for stability and security in relationships. Virgo is practical, detail-oriented, and analytical, while Cancer is intuitive, nurturing, and empathetic. Virgo appreciates Cancer's emotional support and caring nature, while Cancer values Virgo's reliability and attention to detail. Together, they create a harmonious and supportive partnership based on mutual respect and understanding. Communication and emotional expression are important for these two signs to navigate their differences and build a strong connection.

6. Cancer and Libra Compatibility:

Cancer and Libra have complementary qualities that can create a harmonious and balanced relationship. Libra is diplomatic, charming, and sociable, while Cancer is nurturing, intuitive, and empathetic. Libra values harmony and fairness in relationships, which aligns well with Cancer's desire for emotional connection and security. Cancer appreciates Libra's ability to see different perspectives and find compromise, while Libra admires Cancer's empathy and emotional depth. Together, they create a supportive and loving partnership built on mutual understanding and respect. Finding a balance between emotional sensitivity and Libra's need for harmony and balance is key for these two signs to thrive together.

7. Cancer and Scorpio Compatibility:

Cancer and Scorpio share a deep emotional connection and a strong sense of loyalty and commitment in relationships. Scorpio is intense, passionate, and perceptive, while Cancer is nurturing, intuitive, and empathetic. Both signs value emotional depth and intimacy, creating a profound and transformative bond between them. Cancer provides emotional support and understanding, while Scorpio offers depth, intensity, and loyalty. Together, they create a powerful and emotionally fulfilling partnership based on trust and shared values. Honesty, trust, and open communication are essential for these two signs to navigate their intense emotions and build a strong and lasting relationship.

8. Cancer and Sagittarius Compatibility:

Cancer and Sagittarius have contrasting personalities that can lead to both challenges and growth in their relationship. Sagittarius is adventurous, optimistic, and freedom-loving, while Cancer is nurturing, emotional, and home-oriented. Sagittarius may find Cancer too clingy or possessive, while Cancer may feel overwhelmed by Sagittarius' need for independence and exploration. Finding a balance between emotional security and freedom is essential for these two signs to create a harmonious and fulfilling partnership. Building trust, communication, and mutual respect can help Cancer and Sagittarius navigate their differences and create a strong connection.

9. Cancer and Capricorn Compatibility:

Cancer and Capricorn share a strong emotional bond and a desire for security and stability in relationships. Capricorn is ambitious, disciplined, and practical, while Cancer is nurturing, intuitive, and empathetic. Capricorn values hard work, responsibility, and long-term goals, which align well with Cancer's desire for emotional connection and stability. Cancer appreciates Capricorn's reliability and commitment, while Capricorn admires Cancer's emotional depth and intuition. Together, they create a grounded and supportive partnership based on shared values and mutual respect. Balancing emotional sensitivity with Capricorn's practicality and ambition is key for these two signs to thrive together.

10. Cancer and Aquarius Compatibility:

Cancer and Aquarius have contrasting personalities that can create a dynamic and challenging relationship. Aquarius is independent, progressive, and unconventional, while Cancer is nurturing, emotional, and traditional. Aquarius may find Cancer too emotional or clingy, while Cancer may feel overwhelmed by Aquarius' need for freedom and individuality. Finding a balance between emotional depth and independence is essential for these two signs to create a harmonious and fulfilling partnership. Open communication, mutual understanding, and respect for each other's differences can help Cancer and Aquarius navigate their unique dynamics and build a strong connection.

11. Cancer and Pisces Compatibility:
Cancer and Pisces share a deep emotional connection and a strong sense of empathy and intuition in relationships. Pisces is sensitive, imaginative, and compassionate, while Cancer is nurturing, intuitive, and empathetic. Both signs value emotional depth and spiritual connection, creating a profound and soulful bond between them. Cancer provides emotional support and understanding, while Pisces offers creativity, intuition, and compassion. Together, they create a loving and compassionate partnership built on mutual trust and emotional intimacy. Honesty, vulnerability, and emotional expression are essential for these two signs to nurture their connection and create a harmonious and fulfilling relationship.

In conclusion, Cancer's compatibility with other signs varies based on the unique dynamics and qualities of each pairing. By understanding the strengths, challenges, and potential growth opportunities in their relationships, Cancer can navigate their connections with different signs more effectively and create harmonious and fulfilling partnerships. Open communication, mutual respect, and emotional understanding are key for Cancer to build strong and lasting relationships with compatible signs.

Famous Cancer Personalities

Cancer individuals are known for their nurturing and empathetic nature, as well as their deep emotional sensitivity. They are ruled by the Moon, which makes them highly intuitive and connected to their emotions. Famous Cancer personalities often exhibit these traits in their personal and professional lives, making a significant impact on the world with their creativity, compassion, and emotional depth.

One iconic Cancer personality is Princess Diana, born on July 1st. She was known for her grace, compassion, and dedication to humanitarian causes. Diana's emotional intelligence and ability to connect with people from all walks of life made her a beloved figure worldwide. Her philanthropic work, especially in raising awareness about issues like HIV/AIDS and landmines, showcased her caring and nurturing nature.

Another notable Cancer personality is Tom Hanks, born on July 9th. He is celebrated for his versatility as an actor and his ability to portray a wide range of characters with depth and authenticity. Hanks's emotional depth and sensitivity shine through in his performances, earning him multiple awards and widespread acclaim. His roles in films like "Forrest Gump" and "Philadelphia" demonstrate his ability to connect with audiences on a profound emotional level.

Selena Gomez, born on July 22nd, is a prominent Cancer personality known for her talent as a singer, actress, and philanthropist. Gomez's emotional vulnerability and honesty in her music have resonated with fans worldwide. She has also been open about her struggles with mental health, using her platform to raise awareness and advocate for self-care and mental wellness.

Nelson Mandela, born on July 18th, is another famous Cancer personality who left a lasting impact on the world. As a South African anti-apartheid revolutionary and political leader, Mandela fought tirelessly for equality, justice, and human rights. His compassion, forgiveness, and unwavering dedication to peace and reconciliation made him an inspirational figure globally.

Lastly, Meryl Streep, born on June 22nd, is a Cancer personality renowned for her exceptional acting talent and versatility. Streep's ability to embody a wide array of characters with depth and emotional authenticity has earned her numerous accolades, including multiple Academy Awards. Her performances in films like "Sophie's Choice" and "The Iron Lady" showcase her ability to convey complex emotions with nuance and subtlety.

In conclusion, Famous Cancer personalities embody the traits of their zodiac sign, such as emotional depth, compassion, and intuition. Their ability to connect with others on a profound emotional level and make a positive impact on the world showcases the unique strengths of Cancer individuals. Through their creativity, empathy, and dedication, these famous individuals inspire others to embrace their emotions and nurture their own personal growth.

Chapter 6

Leo

Leo Overview and Symbolism

Leo, the fifth sign of the zodiac, is symbolized by the majestic Lion. People born under the sign of Leo are known for their boldness, creativity, and leadership qualities. Leos are ruled by the Sun, the center of our solar system, which symbolizes vitality, energy, and self-expression. This influence makes Leos confident, charismatic, and passionate individuals who often radiate a warm and generous spirit.

Personality Traits of Leo:

Leos are natural-born leaders who possess a strong sense of self-confidence and a magnetic personality. They are ambitious, courageous, and have a deep desire to succeed in all aspects of their lives. Leos are also known for their creativity and love for the spotlight, often excelling in creative fields such as acting, music, or design.

In Love and Relationships:

In relationships, Leos are generous and loving partners who enjoy showering their loved ones with affection and attention. They are loyal and devoted, seeking a deep emotional connection with their partners. However, Leos can also be possessive and demanding at times, needing reassurance of their partner's love and admiration.

Career and Ambitions of Leo:

Leos thrive in leadership roles and excel in careers that allow them to showcase their creativity and talent. They make excellent entrepreneurs, managers, performers, and artists. Leos are driven by ambition and are always looking for opportunities to shine and make a lasting impact in their chosen field.

Strengths and Weaknesses of Leo:

The strengths of Leo lie in their confidence, creativity, and leadership abilities. They are natural-born motivators who inspire those around them to reach their full potential. However, Leos can also be stubborn, arrogant, and overly dramatic at times, needing to learn the importance of humility and compromise.

Leo Compatibility with Other Signs:

Leos are most compatible with signs that appreciate their warmth, generosity, and passion for life. Aries, Sagittarius, and Gemini are ideal matches for Leo, as they share a mutual admiration for each other's strengths and values. Leos may struggle in relationships with signs that are overly critical or controlling, such as Scorpio or Taurus.

Famous Leo Personalities:

Some famous Leo personalities include actors like Jennifer Lawrence and Daniel Radcliffe, musicians like Madonna and Mick Jagger, and leaders like Barack Obama and Nelson Mandela. These individuals embody the charismatic and creative qualities associated with the Leo sign, leaving a lasting impact on the world through their talents and leadership.

In conclusion, Leos are dynamic and charismatic individuals who possess a natural gift for leadership and self-expression. With their confident and creative nature, Leos have the potential to achieve great success in their careers and relationships, leaving a lasting legacy in everything they do.

Personality Traits of Leo

Leo, the fifth sign of the zodiac, is represented by the symbol of the lion. Individuals born under the sign of Leo are known for their charismatic and vibrant personalities. They are ruled by the Sun, which symbolizes vitality, creativity, and a strong sense of self. Leos are natural leaders who exude confidence and have a magnetic presence that draws others towards them.

One of the key personality traits of a Leo is their warm and generous nature. Leos are known for their big hearts and their willingness to go above and beyond to help those they care about. They are loyal and protective of their loved ones, making them fiercely devoted friends and partners.

Leos also possess a strong sense of self-confidence and self-assuredness. They have a natural flair for the dramatic and love being the center of attention. Leos are often the life of the party, with a charismatic and outgoing personality that lights up any room they walk into. They thrive in social settings and enjoy being surrounded by people who appreciate their charm and wit.

Another defining trait of Leos is their creativity and passion. They are natural-born artists who excel in creative pursuits such as music, art, and theater. Leos have a zest for life and a love for all things beautiful. They are often drawn to luxury and opulence, and have a taste for the finer things in life.

Despite their larger-than-life personalities, Leos can also have a stubborn and prideful streak. They can be fiercely independent and may struggle with taking advice or criticism from others. Leos have a strong sense of self-worth and can be sensitive to any perceived slights or challenges to their authority.

In relationships, Leos are passionate and romantic partners. They are loyal and dedicated to their loved ones, showering them with affection and attention. Leos are generous lovers who enjoy spoiling their partners with grand gestures and displays of affection. They thrive in relationships where they feel appreciated and admired.

In their careers, Leos excel in leadership roles where they can showcase their natural charisma and creativity. They are ambitious and driven individuals who are not afraid to take risks in pursuit of their goals. Leos thrive in environments where they can take charge and inspire others with their vision and enthusiasm.

Overall, Leos are vibrant, dynamic individuals who bring a sense of excitement and energy to everything they do. Their warmth, creativity, and passion make them natural-born leaders and beloved friends and partners. Embracing their positive traits while being mindful of their potential pitfalls can help Leos navigate through life with confidence and grace.

Leo in Love and Relationships

Leo, the fifth sign of the zodiac, is ruled by the fiery and passionate Sun. Those born under the sign of Leo are known for their charisma, confidence, and magnetic personality. In love and relationships, Leos are generous, loyal, and affectionate partners who crave admiration and attention.

One of the key traits of a Leo in love is their unwavering loyalty and devotion to their partner. Leos are fiercely protective of their loved ones and will go to great lengths to ensure their happiness and well-being. They are natural leaders who take charge in relationships, often showering their partners with love, affection, and grand gestures.

Leos are known for their romantic nature and love to be the center of attention in their relationships. They enjoy being pampered and adored, and in return, they are generous and affectionate towards their partners. Leos have a strong need for validation and appreciation, and they thrive on compliments and recognition from their loved ones.

In romantic relationships, Leos are passionate and intense lovers who give their all to their partners. They are not afraid to show their emotions and express their love openly and enthusiastically. Leos are often drawn to partners who can match their energy and passion, as they seek a deep and meaningful connection with someone who can keep up with their fiery spirit.

However, Leos can also be prone to jealousy and possessiveness in relationships. They have a strong sense of pride and can be sensitive to any perceived slights or lack of attention from their partners. It is important for Leo to communicate openly and honestly with their partner to avoid misunderstandings and conflicts.

When it comes to compatibility, Leos are most compatible with other fire signs like Aries and Sagittarius, as well as air signs like Gemini and Libra. These signs share Leo's love for excitement, adventure, and intellectual stimulation, making for a harmonious and dynamic relationship.

Famous Leos known for their charismatic and passionate nature include Madonna, Jennifer Lopez, Barack Obama, and Chris Hemsworth. These individuals embody the qualities of a Leo in love – confident, generous, and devoted to their partners.

In conclusion, Leo in love is a passionate and devoted partner who seeks a deep and meaningful connection with someone who can match their energy and intensity. With their romantic nature and desire for admiration, Leos bring excitement and warmth to their relationships, making them loyal and loving companions.

Career and Ambitions of Leo

Leo, the fifth sign of the zodiac, is symbolized by the lion, representing strength, courage, and leadership. Individuals born under the sign of Leo are known for their charismatic and confident nature, making them natural-born leaders. In terms of career and ambitions, Leos are driven by a desire to excel and be recognized for their talents and abilities.

Career Path and Ambitions:

Leos are ambitious individuals who thrive in roles that allow them to take charge and showcase their creative talents. They are drawn to professions where they can be in the spotlight and make a significant impact. Careers in fields such as entertainment, performing arts, fashion, and design appeal to Leos due to their love for creativity and self-expression.

Leos also excel in leadership positions where they can inspire and motivate others. They have a natural ability to command attention and lead with confidence and enthusiasm. Roles in management, entrepreneurship, and public speaking are well-suited for Leos who enjoy being in control and setting high standards for themselves and those around them.

Strengths:

One of the key strengths of Leos in their career is their natural charisma and ability to influence others. They are passionate individuals who are not afraid to pursue their goals and dreams with determination and drive. Leos are also known for their creativity and innovative thinking, which allows them to come up with unique solutions to complex problems.

Another strength of Leos is their ability to take charge and lead with authority. They are confident individuals who are not afraid to step into the spotlight and take on challenging tasks. Leos thrive in high-pressure situations and can handle stress with grace and composure.

Weaknesses:

While Leos have many strengths that contribute to their success in their careers, they may also face challenges due to their tendency to be overly proud and arrogant at times. Their desire for recognition and admiration can sometimes come across as self-centered or egotistical, which may hinder their relationships with colleagues and peers.

Leos may also struggle with delegation and teamwork, as they prefer to take on tasks independently and be in control of the outcome. Learning to collaborate effectively with others and trust in their abilities can help Leos overcome this weakness and achieve greater success in their careers.

Overall, Leos are ambitious individuals with a strong sense of purpose and a drive to succeed in their chosen career paths. By leveraging their natural leadership abilities, creativity, and passion, Leos can carve out successful and fulfilling careers that allow them to shine and make a positive impact in the world.

Strengths and Weaknesses of Leo

Leo, the fifth sign of the zodiac, is represented by the symbol of the lion. People born under the sign of Leo are known for their bold and confident nature. They are ruled by the Sun, which is a symbol of power and vitality. Leos are natural leaders and have a magnetic personality that draws others towards them. In this section, we will dive into the strengths and weaknesses of those born under the sign of Leo.

Strengths of Leo:

1. Leadership Qualities: Leos are born leaders who have a natural ability to take charge and inspire others. They are confident in their decisions and have a strong sense of self-assurance that makes them stand out in any situation.

2. Charismatic and Charming: Leos are known for their charismatic personality and charming demeanor. They have a way of drawing people towards them with their warmth and enthusiasm. Their positive energy is infectious and can uplift those around them.

3. Creative and Passionate: Leos are creative individuals who have a passion for life. They excel in artistic pursuits and enjoy expressing themselves through various forms of creativity. Their passion drives them to pursue their goals with determination and enthusiasm.

4. Generous and Loyal: Leos are generous by nature and are always willing to help those in need. They are fiercely loyal to their loved ones and will go to great lengths to protect and support them. Their loyalty and devotion make them trustworthy and dependable friends and partners.

5. Optimistic and Enthusiastic: Leos have a sunny outlook on life and possess an infectious enthusiasm that inspires others. They have a positive attitude towards challenges and setbacks, always looking for the silver lining in every situation.

Weaknesses of Leo:

1. Stubborn and Egotistical: Leos can sometimes be stubborn and unwilling to consider alternative viewpoints. Their strong sense of self-confidence can lead to ego-driven behavior, making it difficult for them to admit when they are wrong.

2. Attention-Seeking: Leos have a natural desire for attention and admiration. They can come across as self-centered or attention-seeking at times, seeking validation and praise from others to boost their ego.

3. Impulsive and Dramatic: Leos are known for their dramatic flair and can sometimes be prone to impulsiveness. They may act on emotions without considering the consequences, leading to hasty decisions or conflicts with others.

4. Arrogant and Domineering: Leos can sometimes come across as arrogant or domineering due to their strong personality and need for control. They may inadvertently intimidate others with their authoritative demeanor, leading to power struggles in relationships.

5. Sensitive to Criticism: Despite their confident exterior, Leos can be sensitive to criticism and may take feedback personally. They have a deep need for validation and approval, making them vulnerable to feeling hurt or insecure when their actions are questioned.

In conclusion, Leos possess a unique blend of strengths and weaknesses that shape their personalities and interactions with others. By understanding and embracing these traits, Leos can harness their strengths to lead fulfilling lives while working on overcoming their weaknesses to cultivate personal growth and self-awareness.

Leo Compatibility with Other Signs

Leo, the confident and charismatic sign ruled by the Sun, is known for its bold and passionate nature. People born under the sign of Leo are natural leaders who crave attention and admiration. When it comes to relationships, Leos are generous, loyal, and protective partners who seek a deep and meaningful connection with their loved ones. Let's explore how Leo's fiery energy interacts with the other zodiac signs in terms of compatibility:

Aries (March 21 - April 19):

Leo and Aries share a dynamic and energetic bond. Both signs are fire signs, which means they understand each other's need for excitement and adventure. Their relationship is filled with passion, creativity, and a strong sense of loyalty. However, both signs can be dominant and have strong personalities, which may lead to power struggles if not managed properly.

Taurus (April 20 - May 20):

Leo and Taurus have a magnetic attraction based on their shared love for luxury and comfort. Leo's warmth and Taurus's stability create a harmonious partnership where both signs feel secure and appreciated. However, Leo's need for attention and Taurus's stubbornness can sometimes clash, requiring compromise and understanding from both sides.

Gemini (May 21 - June 20):

Leo and Gemini form a fun and intellectually stimulating duo. Both signs are social butterflies who enjoy engaging in lively conversations and exploring new ideas. Leo's confidence complements Gemini's adaptability, creating a dynamic relationship filled with laughter and excitement. However, Leo's desire for loyalty and commitment may clash with Gemini's need for freedom and variety.

Cancer (June 21 - July 22):

Leo and Cancer create a nurturing and supportive bond where Leo provides strength and protection while Cancer offers emotional depth and sensitivity. Leo's warmth and generosity help Cancer come out of their shell, while Cancer's intuition and understanding provide comfort and security for Leo. However, Leo's need for attention and Cancer's moodiness may create challenges that require open communication and compromise.

Virgo (August 23 - September 22):

Leo and Virgo have contrasting personalities that can either complement or clash with each other. Leo's passion and creativity are balanced by Virgo's practicality and attention to detail. While Leo thrives on spontaneity and grand gestures, Virgo values stability and reliability. Finding a middle ground and appreciating each other's strengths is key to a successful Leo-Virgo relationship.

Libra (September 23 - October 22):

Leo and Libra form a harmonious and balanced partnership based on mutual respect and admiration. Both signs value beauty, harmony, and social connections, creating a strong foundation for a loving and supportive relationship. Leo's confidence and Libra's charm complement each other, making them a dynamic and sociable couple. However, Leo's need for attention and Libra's indecisiveness may require patience and understanding to navigate.

Scorpio (October 23 - November 21):

Leo and Scorpio share a passionate and intense connection that is both challenging and transformative. Both signs are strong-willed and fiercely loyal, creating a deep and powerful bond. However, Leo's need for admiration and Scorpio's possessiveness can lead to power struggles and conflicts if not addressed. Trust, communication, and mutual respect are essential for Leo and Scorpio to navigate their differences and build a strong foundation for their relationship.

Sagittarius (November 22 - December 21):

Leo and Sagittarius are kindred spirits who share a love for adventure, freedom, and optimism. Both signs are passionate, energetic, and enthusiastic, creating a dynamic and exciting partnership. Leo's generosity and warmth complement Sagittarius's adventurous spirit, making them a fun-loving and adventurous couple. However, Leo's need for attention and Sagittarius's love for independence may require compromise and open communication to maintain a harmonious relationship.

Capricorn (December 22 - January 19):

Leo and Capricorn have contrasting personalities that can either complement or clash with each other. Leo's outgoing and expressive nature is balanced by Capricorn's practicality and ambition. While Leo seeks recognition and admiration, Capricorn values hard work and determination. Finding a balance between Leo's need for attention and Capricorn's focus on responsibility and structure is crucial for building a strong and lasting relationship.

Aquarius (January 20 - February 18):
Leo and Aquarius create a dynamic and intellectually stimulating bond based on mutual respect and admiration. Both signs are independent, creative, and forward-thinking, which makes them a unique and innovative couple. Leo's warmth and generosity complement Aquarius's humanitarian ideals, creating a harmonious partnership filled with excitement and growth. However, Leo's desire for attention and Aquarius's need for freedom and independence may require compromise and understanding to maintain a healthy relationship.

Pisces (February 19 - March 20):
Leo and Pisces form a compassionate and romantic pairing where Leo's strength and confidence provide a sense of security for sensitive Pisces. Both signs are creative, intuitive, and emotional, creating a deep and empathetic connection. Leo's generosity and Pisces's empathy make them a caring and supportive couple. However, Leo's need for attention and Pisces's tendency towards escapism may require patience and understanding to overcome potential challenges and build a strong foundation for their relationship.

In conclusion, Leo's compatibility with other signs is influenced by a combination of factors including shared values, communication styles, and emotional needs. While Leo's warmth, generosity, and passion make them charismatic and captivating partners, understanding and respecting the differences and similarities between Leo and their partners are essential for building a harmonious and fulfilling relationship. By embracing their strengths and working through challenges with patience and empathy, Leo can create lasting and meaningful connections with a wide range of zodiac signs.

Famous Leo Personalities

Leo, the fifth sign of the zodiac, is represented by the symbol of the lion. Leos are known for their charismatic and confident personalities, often taking on leadership roles with ease. They are ruled by the Sun, which bestows upon them a sense of warmth, creativity, and vitality. Famous Leo personalities embody these characteristics and have made significant contributions in various fields. Let's explore some of the most notable individuals born under the sign of Leo:

1. Barack Obama (August 4, 1961): The 44th President of the United States, Barack Obama, is a quintessential Leo. Known for his powerful presence, eloquence, and leadership qualities, Obama inspired millions with his message of hope and change.

2. Madonna (August 16, 1958): The "Queen of Pop," Madonna, is a Leo icon known for her bold and innovative approach to music and fashion. Her fiery personality and fearless attitude have solidified her status as a music legend.

3. Jennifer Lopez (July 24, 1969): Actress, singer, and businesswoman Jennifer Lopez is a Leo powerhouse. Known for her glamour, confidence, and versatility, Lopez has achieved success in multiple industries and continues to inspire women around the world.

4. Arnold Schwarzenegger (July 30, 1947): Actor and former Governor of California, Arnold Schwarzenegger, is a Leo known for his larger-than-life persona and determination. His career in bodybuilding, Hollywood, and politics reflects the ambitious nature of Leos.

5. Coco Chanel (August 19, 1883): Fashion icon Coco Chanel, born under the sign of Leo, revolutionized the world of fashion with her timeless designs and bold aesthetic. Her creative vision and fearless spirit continue to influence the industry today.

6. Sandra Bullock (July 26, 1964): Academy Award-winning actress Sandra Bullock embodies the grace, charm, and strength commonly associated with Leos. Her versatile performances have earned her critical acclaim and a place among Hollywood's elite.

7. Ben Affleck (August 15, 1972): Actor, director, and producer Ben Affleck is a Leo known for his passion for storytelling and filmmaking. His dedication to his craft and ability to lead both in front of and behind the camera showcase the natural leadership qualities of Leos.

8. Halle Berry (August 14, 1966): Actress Halle Berry, the first African-American woman to win an Academy Award for Best Actress, is a Leo known for her talent, beauty, and resilience. Her bold choices in film roles and advocacy work reflect the courage and determination of Leos.

9. Chris Hemsworth (August 11, 1983): Australian actor Chris Hemsworth, best known for his portrayal of Thor in the Marvel Cinematic Universe, embodies the strength, charisma, and magnetism of a Leo. His commanding presence on screen and off has made him a global superstar.

10. Daniel Radcliffe (July 23, 1989): Actor Daniel Radcliffe, famous for his role as Harry Potter, is a Leo known for his dedication to his craft and humble demeanor. His ability to balance fame with authenticity reflects the grounded nature of Leos.

These famous Leo personalities exemplify the leadership, creativity, and passion that define this dynamic zodiac sign. Their achievements serve as a testament to the influence of astrology in shaping personalities and guiding individuals towards success.

Chapter 7

Virgo

Virgo Overview and Symbolism

Virgo is the sixth sign of the zodiac, symbolized by the Virgin. People born under this sign are known for their analytical and practical nature. Virgos are ruled by the planet Mercury, which is associated with communication and intellect. They belong to the Earth element, along with Taurus and Capricorn, which signifies their grounded and reliable personality traits.

Symbolism:

The symbol of Virgo, the Virgin, represents purity, innocence, and a sense of modesty. It also symbolizes a sense of duty, service, and attention to detail. Virgos are known for their meticulous nature, as they pay attention to even the smallest of details in everything they do.

Personality Traits of Virgo:

Virgos are known for their practicality, attention to detail, and strong work ethic. They are highly organized and methodical in their approach to tasks, making them reliable and efficient workers. Virgos are also known for their analytical abilities and critical thinking skills, which make them excellent problem solvers.

Virgo in Love and Relationships:

In relationships, Virgos are loyal and dedicated partners. They value honesty and communication in their relationships and are known for their supportive and caring nature. However, Virgos can be overly critical at times, expecting perfection from themselves and their partners.

Career and Ambitions of Virgo:

Virgos excel in careers that require precision, organization, and attention to detail. They make great accountants, editors, writers, analysts, and healthcare professionals. Virgos are hardworking and dedicated to their work, always striving for perfection in everything they do.

Strengths and Weaknesses of Virgo:
Some of the strengths of Virgos include their analytical abilities, attention to detail, and practical nature. They are reliable, hardworking, and dedicated individuals. However, Virgos can also be overly critical, perfectionistic, and prone to worrying too much about minor details.

Virgo Compatibility with Other Signs:
Virgos are most compatible with Taurus, Capricorn, Cancer, and Scorpio. Taurus and Capricorn share Virgo's practical and grounded nature, while Cancer and Scorpio provide emotional depth and understanding to Virgo's analytical approach to life.

Famous Virgo Personalities:
Some famous Virgos include Beyoncé, Freddie Mercury, Mother Teresa, Tim Burton, and Amy Winehouse. These individuals showcase the diverse talents and characteristics of the Virgo sign, from creativity and dedication to service and perfectionism.

In conclusion, Virgo is a sign characterized by its practicality, attention to detail, and analytical nature. People born under this sign are hardworking, reliable, and dedicated individuals who excel in careers that require precision and organization. While Virgos may struggle with perfectionism and critical tendencies, they also possess a strong sense of duty and service that makes them invaluable in both personal and professional relationships.

Personality Traits of Virgo

Virgo, the sixth sign of the zodiac, is represented by the symbol of the Maiden, signifying purity, modesty, and practicality. Those born under the sign of Virgo are known for their meticulous attention to detail, analytical mindset, and strong sense of responsibility. Let's delve deeper into the personality traits that characterize Virgo individuals.

One of the key traits of a Virgo is their perfectionism. They have a keen eye for detail and strive for excellence in everything they do. Virgos are highly organized and methodical, preferring structure and order in their lives. They are known for their precision and efficiency, making them excellent at tasks that require accuracy and attention to detail.

Virgos are also known for their practicality and pragmatism. They approach life with a logical and rational mindset, always seeking practical solutions to problems. Virgos are great problem-solvers and excel at finding efficient ways to navigate challenges. Their analytical nature allows them to assess situations objectively and make well-informed decisions.

Another prominent trait of Virgos is their strong sense of responsibility. They take their commitments seriously and are reliable and dependable individuals. Virgos are known for their work ethic and dedication to their responsibilities, whether it be in their professional or personal lives. They are diligent workers who take pride in their ability to get things done efficiently and effectively.

In addition to their practical and responsible nature, Virgos are also known for their modesty and humility. Despite their many talents and accomplishments, Virgos are not ones to boast or seek attention. They are humble individuals who prefer to let their actions speak for themselves. Virgos are also known for their caring and nurturing nature, always willing to lend a helping hand to those in need.

On the flip side, Virgos can sometimes be overly critical of themselves and others. Their perfectionist tendencies can lead them to be overly self-critical and nit-pick at minor flaws. Virgos may also have high standards for those around them, which can sometimes come across as judgmental. It's important for Virgos to learn to balance their desire for perfection with acceptance and understanding.

In relationships, Virgos are loyal and devoted partners who value honesty and communication. They are attentive to the needs of their loved ones and strive to create harmonious and stable relationships. Virgos may struggle with expressing their emotions openly, but their actions often speak louder than words.

Overall, Virgos are practical, meticulous, and responsible individuals who bring a sense of order and efficiency to everything they do. Their attention to detail, analytical mindset, and strong work ethic make them valuable assets in both their personal and professional lives. By embracing their strengths and working on their weaknesses, Virgos can continue to grow and thrive in all aspects of their lives.

Virgo in Love and Relationships

Virgos are known for their practical and analytical approach to life, and this extends to their relationships as well. When it comes to love, Virgos are loyal, caring, and devoted partners who value stability and commitment. They are meticulous in their attention to detail and have high standards for themselves and their partners. Let's delve deeper into how Virgos approach love and relationships:

Personality Traits of Virgo in Love:
In love, Virgos are thoughtful and considerate partners who show their affection through acts of service and attention to detail. They are not ones for grand gestures or dramatic displays of love but prefer to express their feelings through practical gestures that show they care. Virgos are reliable and dependable, making them great partners who can be counted on in times of need.

Virgo Compatibility with Other Signs:
Virgos are most compatible with signs that share their practical and grounded approach to life, such as Taurus and Capricorn. These signs understand Virgo's need for stability and appreciate their attention to detail. Virgos may also find compatibility with water signs like Cancer and Scorpio, who can provide emotional depth and sensitivity to balance out Virgo's rational nature.

Strengths and Weaknesses in Relationships:
One of Virgo's strengths in relationships is their ability to communicate effectively and solve problems with a logical approach. They are good listeners and strive to understand their partner's needs and concerns. However, Virgos can be overly critical at times, pointing out flaws and imperfections in themselves and others. This tendency can lead to feelings of inadequacy in their partners if not managed properly.

Virgo in Love and Romance:
In romantic relationships, Virgos are devoted and caring partners who prioritize the well-being of their loved ones. They may struggle with expressing their emotions openly but show their love through practical gestures and acts of service. Virgos value stability and security in relationships and seek partners who share their values and goals for the future.

Career and Ambitions of Virgo:
In their careers, Virgos are driven and detail-oriented individuals who excel in roles that require precision and organization. They are analytical thinkers who thrive in environments where their skills and expertise are valued. Virgos may pursue careers in fields such as healthcare, education, or research, where their meticulous nature and problem-solving abilities can shine.

Famous Virgo Personalities:
Some famous Virgos known for their analytical minds and attention to detail include Beyoncé, Keanu Reeves, and Tim Burton. These individuals exemplify the traits of Virgo in their professional endeavors and personal lives, showcasing the dedication and precision that are hallmarks of this zodiac sign.

In conclusion, Virgos approach love and relationships with a practical and thoughtful mindset, valuing loyalty, commitment, and stability above all else. Their attention to detail and analytical nature make them reliable partners who excel in communication and problem-solving. By understanding and embracing their strengths and weaknesses, Virgos can cultivate fulfilling and harmonious relationships that stand the test of time.

Career and Ambitions of Virgo

Virgos are known for their analytical and detail-oriented nature, making them well-suited for careers that require precision, organization, and problem-solving skills. In the professional world, Virgos are often valued for their meticulous approach to work and their ability to spot errors or inefficiencies that others may overlook. Let's delve deeper into the career and ambitions of Virgo individuals.

Career Choices:
Virgos are drawn to careers that allow them to use their keen analytical skills and attention to detail. They excel in roles that involve research, data analysis, accounting, editing, writing, and other tasks that require a methodical and systematic approach. Virgos are also well-suited for professions in healthcare, particularly as nurses, doctors, or therapists, where their compassionate nature and dedication to helping others shine through.

Ambitions:
Virgos are ambitious individuals who strive for excellence in everything they do. They set high standards for themselves and are constantly seeking ways to

improve and grow in their chosen field. Virgos are not content with mediocrity and are always pushing themselves to achieve greater levels of success. Their ambitious nature drives them to take on new challenges and responsibilities, as they are always looking for ways to expand their skills and knowledge.

Work Ethic:
Virgos are known for their strong work ethic and dedication to their craft. They are reliable and conscientious employees who take pride in their work and strive for perfection in everything they do. Virgos are not afraid to put in the hard work and long hours necessary to achieve their goals. They are disciplined and focused individuals who approach their tasks with a sense of purpose and determination.

Career Success Strategies:
To achieve success in their careers, Virgos should focus on honing their analytical skills, attention to detail, and organizational abilities. They should seek out opportunities that allow them to showcase their talents in problem-solving, planning, and executing tasks with precision. Virgos should also prioritize self-care and work-life balance to prevent burnout and maintain their mental and physical well-being.

Finding Fulfillment:
Virgos find fulfillment in careers that allow them to make a meaningful impact, whether it be through helping others, contributing to a greater cause, or achieving personal growth and development. They thrive in environments that appreciate their meticulous approach to work and provide them with opportunities for growth and advancement. Virgos should seek out roles that align with their values and allow them to utilize their skills and talents to the fullest.

In conclusion, Virgos are driven and ambitious individuals who excel in careers that require analytical thinking, attention to detail, and a strong work ethic. By leveraging their natural strengths and focusing on personal growth and development, Virgos can achieve great success and fulfillment in their professional lives.

Strengths and Weaknesses of Virgo

Virgos, born between August 23 and September 22, are known for their meticulous attention to detail, practical approach to life, and analytical mindset. In this section, we will delve into the strengths and weaknesses of individuals belonging to the Virgo zodiac sign.

Strengths:

1. Analytical and Detail-Oriented: Virgos possess a keen eye for detail and are excellent at analyzing situations. They excel in tasks that require precision and thoroughness, making them valuable assets in professions that demand accuracy.

2. Practical and Organized: Virgos are known for their practicality and organizational skills. They have a methodical approach to life and are adept at planning and managing tasks efficiently.

3. Reliable and Hardworking: Virgos are dedicated and reliable individuals who take their responsibilities seriously. They are hardworking and committed to achieving their goals, making them dependable team members and colleagues.

4. Intelligent and Perceptive: Virgos have sharp intellects and a deep sense of intuition. They can quickly grasp complex concepts and are skilled at problem-solving and finding practical solutions to challenges.

5. Caring and Supportive: Despite their analytical nature, Virgos are compassionate and caring individuals. They are always willing to lend a helping hand to those in need and offer practical advice and support to friends and family.

Weaknesses:

1. Overcritical and Perfectionistic: One of the key weaknesses of Virgos is their tendency to be overly critical, both of themselves and others. They have high standards and can be perfectionists, which may lead to feelings of dissatisfaction and frustration.

2. Pessimistic and Worrisome: Virgos have a tendency to worry excessively and can be prone to negative thinking. Their analytical minds often focus on potential problems and worst-case scenarios, leading to anxiety and stress.

3. Rigid and Inflexible: Virgos can be rigid in their thinking and resistant to change. They prefer structure and order in their lives, which can make them uncomfortable with uncertainty and new situations.

4. Self-Critical and Self-Doubting: Virgos can be overly self-critical and have a tendency to doubt their abilities. They may struggle with self-esteem issues and have a hard time acknowledging their own accomplishments.

5. Critical of Others: Due to their high standards and attention to detail, Virgos can be critical of others as well. They may come across as nitpicky or judgmental, which can strain relationships and lead to misunderstandings.

In conclusion, Virgos are intelligent, practical, and caring individuals with a strong sense of responsibility. While their attention to detail and analytical skills are valuable assets, they may need to work on managing their critical tendencies and perfectionistic traits to achieve a greater sense of balance and well-being in their lives. Understanding and embracing both their strengths and weaknesses can help Virgos navigate challenges and harness their full potential.

Virgo Compatibility with Other Signs

Virgo, the sixth sign of the zodiac, is known for its analytical and practical nature. People born under this sign are detail-oriented, organized, and value precision in all aspects of their lives. When it comes to relationships, Virgos seek harmony, stability, and intellectual stimulation. Let's explore how Virgo's traits interact with other zodiac signs in terms of compatibility:

1. Aries (March 21 - April 19):
Virgo and Aries have contrasting personalities. Aries is spontaneous and impulsive, while Virgo is methodical and cautious. While Aries may find Virgo too critical, Virgo may see Aries as too reckless. However, if they can appreciate each other's strengths and learn from their differences, they can complement each other well.

2. Taurus (April 20 - May 20):

Virgo and Taurus share a practical and grounded approach to life. Both signs value stability, loyalty, and commitment in relationships. They understand each other's need for security and can build a strong foundation based on mutual respect and trust. Their shared values can lead to a harmonious and fulfilling partnership.

3. Gemini (May 21 - June 20):

Virgo and Gemini have different communication styles. Virgo is detail-oriented and prefers practical conversations, while Gemini is more playful and enjoys intellectual debates. Despite these differences, they can learn from each other's strengths. Virgo can help Gemini focus and follow through on their ideas, while Gemini can encourage Virgo to be more flexible and open-minded.

4. Cancer (June 21 - July 22):

Virgo and Cancer are both nurturing signs that value emotional connection and security in relationships. They can create a warm and supportive environment for each other. Virgo's analytical skills can complement Cancer's intuition, leading to a balanced partnership. However, Virgo's tendency to be critical may clash with Cancer's sensitivity, so open communication is key.

5. Leo (July 23 - August 22):

Virgo and Leo have different approaches to life and relationships. Leo is confident, charismatic, and enjoys being the center of attention, while Virgo is humble, practical, and detail-oriented. Despite these differences, they can learn to appreciate each other's strengths. Virgo can help Leo stay grounded and focused, while Leo can inspire Virgo to be more spontaneous and adventurous.

6. Libra (September 23 - October 22):

Virgo and Libra share a love for harmony, balance, and beauty. They both value fairness and diplomacy in relationships. Libra's charm and social skills can complement Virgo's analytical abilities. Together, they can create a harmonious and aesthetically pleasing partnership. However, Virgo may need to be mindful of Libra's indecisiveness, while Libra may need to understand Virgo's need for order and structure.

7. Scorpio (October 23 - November 21):

Virgo and Scorpio have a deep emotional connection and intense bond. Both signs are passionate, loyal, and committed in relationships. They share a desire for authenticity and depth in their interactions. Virgo's practicality can balance Scorpio's intensity, leading to a strong and transformative partnership. However, Virgo may need to be more open to Scorpio's emotional depth, while Scorpio may need to respect Virgo's need for personal space.

8. Sagittarius (November 22 - December 21):

Virgo and Sagittarius have different approaches to life and relationships. Sagittarius is adventurous, optimistic, and freedom-loving, while Virgo is practical, detail-oriented, and cautious. While they may have contrasting personalities, they can learn from each other's perspectives. Virgo can help Sagittarius focus on the details and follow through on their ideas, while Sagittarius can inspire Virgo to be more open-minded and spontaneous.

In conclusion, Virgo's compatibility with other signs varies based on how well they can understand and appreciate each other's differences. By embracing their unique qualities and working together to overcome challenges, Virgo can build strong and fulfilling relationships with a wide range of zodiac signs.

Famous Virgo Personalities

Virgos are known for their analytical and practical nature, as well as their attention to detail and organizational skills. They are ruled by Mercury, the planet of communication and intellect, which gives them a sharp mind and a keen ability to solve problems. Famous Virgo personalities exhibit these traits in various aspects of their lives, from their careers to their personal relationships.

One of the most iconic Virgo personalities is Beyoncé Knowles. Born on September 4th, Beyoncé is a multi-talented singer, songwriter, and actress known for her powerful vocals and captivating performances. Her meticulous attention to detail and perfectionism have helped her achieve massive success in the music industry, earning her numerous awards and accolades.

Another notable Virgo is Mother Teresa, born on August 26th. Her selfless dedication to helping the poor and marginalized in society exemplifies the compassionate and service-oriented nature of Virgos. Mother Teresa's humility, kindness, and unwavering commitment to her humanitarian work have inspired millions around the world.

On the political front, Angela Merkel, born on July 17th, is a prominent Virgo personality known for her leadership as the Chancellor of Germany. Merkel's analytical approach to governance and her pragmatic decision-making have earned her respect both domestically and internationally. Her attention to detail and ability to navigate complex political landscapes have solidified her reputation as a formidable leader.

In the world of literature, Roald Dahl, born on September 13th, stands out as a celebrated Virgo author known for his imaginative storytelling and quirky characters. Dahl's meticulous craftmanship and keen eye for detail have made his works beloved classics that continue to captivate readers of all ages.

In the realm of sports, Kobe Bryant, born on August 23rd, was a legendary basketball player known for his relentless work ethic and attention to detail on the court. Bryant's dedication to his craft and his pursuit of excellence epitomize the Virgo commitment to continuous improvement and mastery.

These famous Virgo personalities demonstrate the diverse ways in which Virgo traits manifest in individuals across various fields. From creative pursuits to humanitarian efforts, from leadership roles to athletic achievements, Virgos showcase their analytical abilities, attention to detail, and commitment to excellence in all that they do. Their influence serves as a testament to the power of the Virgo spirit in shaping the world around us.

Chapter 8

Libra

Libra Overview and Symbolism

Libra is the seventh sign of the zodiac, represented by the symbol of the scales. Libras are known for their sense of balance, harmony, and fairness. They are ruled by the planet Venus, which influences their love of beauty, art, and aesthetics. Libras are diplomatic and sociable individuals who value peace and relationships.

Symbolism:

The symbol of the scales represents Libra's desire for balance and justice. Libras strive to maintain equilibrium in all aspects of their lives, seeking harmony and avoiding conflict whenever possible. They are known for their ability to see both sides of a situation and make decisions that are fair and just.

Personality Traits:

Libras are charming and charismatic individuals who excel in social situations. They are natural peacemakers, always seeking to find common ground and resolve conflicts. Libras are known for their diplomatic nature and ability to see things from different perspectives. They have a strong sense of justice and fairness, often standing up for what they believe is right.

Love and Relationships:

In love and relationships, Libras are romantic and idealistic. They value partnership and seek harmony and balance in their relationships. Libras are loyal and devoted partners who prioritize communication and compromise. They are known for their ability to create a peaceful and harmonious atmosphere in their relationships.

Career and Ambitions:

Libras are drawn to careers that allow them to express their creativity and sense of beauty. They excel in fields such as art, design, fashion, and diplomacy. Libras are skilled communicators and excel in roles that require negotiation and mediation. They are also drawn to professions that involve promoting harmony and justice.

Strengths and Weaknesses:
Libras are known for their charm, diplomacy, and ability to see multiple perspectives. They are excellent communicators and have a strong sense of fairness and justice. However, Libras can struggle with indecision and may avoid confrontation at all costs. They may also have a tendency to be overly idealistic and may struggle to set boundaries in their relationships.

Compatibility with Other Signs:
Libras are most compatible with signs that share their love of beauty, harmony, and balance. They get along well with Gemini, Aquarius, and other Libras. They may struggle in relationships with more assertive signs like Aries and Capricorn, as they may find it challenging to assert themselves and maintain their sense of balance.

Famous Libra Personalities:
Some famous Libras include Kim Kardashian, Serena Williams, Will Smith, and Gwyneth Paltrow. These individuals exemplify Libra traits such as charm, diplomacy, and a love of beauty and aesthetics.

In conclusion, Libras are diplomatic and harmonious individuals who value balance, justice, and relationships. They excel in roles that require communication, negotiation, and creativity, and strive to create a peaceful and harmonious atmosphere in all aspects of their lives.

Personality Traits of Libra

Libra, the seventh sign of the zodiac, is symbolized by the scales, representing balance, harmony, and justice. People born under the sign of Libra are known for their diplomatic nature, charming personality, and strong sense of fairness. Here is a detailed look at the personality traits of Libra individuals:

1. Diplomatic: Libras are natural peacemakers and are skilled at resolving conflicts with their diplomatic approach. They have a knack for seeing both sides of an issue and are adept at finding compromises that satisfy everyone involved.

2. Charming: One of the most notable traits of Libras is their charm and charisma. They have a way of captivating others with their grace, wit, and social finesse. Libras are often the life of the party and have a magnetic personality that draws people to them.

3. Fair-minded: Libras have a strong sense of justice and fairness. They believe in equality and strive to create a harmonious environment where everyone is treated with respect and consideration. Libras can be relied upon to make decisions that are fair and balanced.

4. Social: Libras are social butterflies who thrive in social settings. They enjoy connecting with others, making new friends, and engaging in lively conversations. Libras are natural networkers and excel in building relationships with people from all walks of life.

5. Indecisive: One of the challenges that Libras face is their tendency to be indecisive. Because they can see multiple perspectives, Libras may struggle to make decisions quickly and may weigh all options before committing to a choice. This can sometimes lead to indecision and procrastination.

6. Harmony-seeking: Libras are peace-loving individuals who strive to create harmony in their relationships and surroundings. They avoid conflict and discord whenever possible and work hard to maintain a sense of balance and equilibrium in their lives.

7. Aesthetic: Libras have a strong appreciation for beauty and aesthetics. They are drawn to art, design, and all things visually pleasing. Libras have a keen eye for style and often have a knack for creating elegant and tasteful environments.

8. People-pleasers: Libras have a tendency to prioritize the needs and desires of others over their own. They are natural caregivers and often go out of their way to make others happy. While this trait can be admirable, it is important for Libras to also prioritize self-care and set boundaries in their relationships.

In conclusion, Libras are known for their diplomatic, charming, and fair-minded nature. They excel in social situations, value harmony and balance, and have a keen appreciation for beauty. While they may struggle with indecision at times and have a tendency to prioritize others over themselves, Libras bring a sense of grace and harmony to the world around them.

Libra in Love and Relationships

Libra, the seventh sign of the zodiac, is symbolized by the scales, representing balance, harmony, and justice. People born under the sign of Libra are known for their charm, diplomacy, and love for beauty and aesthetics. In love and relationships, Libras are romantic, sociable, and seek harmony and partnership.

Libras are natural lovers of love, and they thrive in relationships where there is mutual respect, understanding, and compromise. They are known for their ability to see both sides of a situation, making them excellent mediators and peacemakers in their relationships. Libras value fairness and equality, and they strive to create a harmonious and balanced partnership with their significant other.

When it comes to love, Libras are often drawn to partners who are intelligent, charming, and emotionally balanced. They appreciate good conversation and intellectual stimulation in their relationships. Libras are also attracted to people who share their love for beauty, art, and culture, as they enjoy indulging in romantic experiences that stimulate their senses.

In relationships, Libras are attentive and caring partners who go out of their way to make their loved ones feel special and appreciated. They are known for their romantic gestures, thoughtful gifts, and ability to create a sense of elegance and luxury in their relationships. Libras value partnership and companionship, and they are happiest when they are in a loving and harmonious relationship.

However, Libras can sometimes struggle with decision-making in relationships, as they can be indecisive and have a tendency to avoid conflict. They may also have a fear of confrontation, which can lead them to suppress their true feelings and needs in order to maintain peace and harmony in their relationships. It is important for Libras to learn to assert themselves and communicate openly and honestly with their partners in order to create a healthy and fulfilling relationship.

In terms of compatibility, Libras are most compatible with fellow air signs like Gemini and Aquarius, as they share a similar intellectual and communicative nature. Libras also get along well with fire signs like Leo and Sagittarius, who bring passion and excitement into their lives. Additionally, Libras can find balance and harmony in relationships with other cardinal signs like Aries, Cancer, and Capricorn.

Famous Libra personalities such as Will Smith, Kim Kardashian, and John Lennon exemplify the charm, charisma, and grace that are characteristic of this sign. Overall, Libras are idealistic and romantic partners who seek to create a harmonious and loving relationship built on mutual respect, communication, and compromise.

Career and Ambitions of Libra

Libra, the Balancer, is the seventh sign of the zodiac and is represented by the symbol of the Scales. People born under the sign of Libra are known for their diplomatic nature, charm, and ability to see both sides of a situation. When it comes to career and ambitions, Libras are driven by a desire for harmony, justice, and beauty in all aspects of their professional lives.

Libras excel in careers that allow them to use their excellent communication skills and natural ability to negotiate and mediate. They are often drawn to professions in law, diplomacy, mediation, and counseling, where their fair-mindedness and ability to see multiple perspectives are highly valued. Libras are skilled at finding common ground and working towards compromise, making them excellent team players and leaders in collaborative environments.

One of the key ambitions of Libras is to create a sense of balance and harmony in their work environment. They are often motivated by a desire to create a peaceful and aesthetically pleasing workspace that fosters creativity and productivity. Libras have a keen eye for design and beauty, and they thrive in professions that allow them to express their creativity, such as interior design, fashion, or the arts.

In addition to their creative talents, Libras are also highly analytical and strategic thinkers. They are adept at weighing all options before making decisions and are skilled at problem-solving and finding innovative solutions.

Libras are not afraid to take on challenges and are motivated by the opportunity to learn and grow in their careers.

When it comes to ambition, Libras are driven by a desire to achieve success and recognition in their chosen field. They are dedicated and hardworking individuals who are willing to put in the effort to reach their goals. Libras value fairness and justice, and they are passionate about making a positive impact in the world through their work.

In terms of strengths, Libras are known for their ability to maintain a calm and composed demeanor even in stressful situations. They are excellent communicators and are skilled at building relationships with colleagues and clients. Libras are also highly adaptable and can thrive in diverse work environments.

However, like all signs, Libras also have their weaknesses. They can sometimes be indecisive and struggle with making firm decisions. Libras may also have a tendency to avoid conflict and confrontation, which can sometimes hinder their ability to assert themselves in the workplace.

Overall, Libras are driven by a desire for balance, harmony, and beauty in their careers. They excel in professions that allow them to use their diplomatic skills, creativity, and strategic thinking to make a positive impact in the world. With their dedication and hard work, Libras can achieve great success and fulfillment in their chosen career paths.

Strengths and Weaknesses of Libra

Libras are known for their diplomatic and fair-minded nature, making them excellent mediators and peacemakers in both personal and professional relationships. They are ruled by Venus, the planet of love and beauty, which influences their desire for harmony and balance in all aspects of their lives. Libras are represented by the scales, symbolizing their innate sense of justice and desire for equality. In this section, we will explore the strengths and weaknesses of Libra individuals in more detail.

Strengths of Libra:

1. Diplomatic: Libras are known for their ability to see all sides of a situation and make fair and balanced decisions. They excel at resolving conflicts and finding compromises that satisfy all parties involved.

2. Charming: Libras have a natural charm and charisma that draws people to them. They are social butterflies who enjoy engaging with others and forming meaningful connections.

3. Romantic: Ruled by Venus, Libras are hopeless romantics who appreciate beauty, love, and romance. They are attentive partners who strive to create harmonious and loving relationships.

4. Cooperative: Libras are team players who work well in group settings. They value collaboration and are willing to put the needs of the group above their own individual desires.

5. Stylish: Libras have a keen eye for aesthetics and enjoy surrounding themselves with beauty. They have a flair for fashion and design, often cultivating a refined and elegant personal style.

Weaknesses of Libra:

1. Indecisive: Libras can struggle with making decisions, as they tend to weigh all options carefully before committing to a choice. Their desire for balance and harmony can sometimes lead to indecisiveness and procrastination.

2. People-pleasers: Libras have a strong desire to please others and avoid conflict at all costs. This can sometimes lead them to prioritize the needs of others over their own well-being, leading to feelings of resentment or burnout.

3. Superficial: Libras can be overly focused on appearances and superficial qualities, sometimes neglecting deeper emotional connections. They may prioritize surface-level attributes over substance in their relationships.

4. Avoid confrontation: Libras have a strong aversion to conflict and may go to great lengths to avoid confrontation. This can lead to unresolved issues simmering beneath the surface and causing tension in their relationships.

5. Indecisive: Libras can be prone to indecisiveness, especially when faced with conflicting options or opinions. This can result in delays or missed opportunities if they are unable to make firm decisions.

Overall, Libras are known for their charming personality, diplomatic nature, and desire for harmony. While they possess many strengths that make them excellent partners and friends, they may also struggle with indecisiveness, people-pleasing tendencies, and a fear of confrontation. By understanding and balancing these traits, Libras can harness their strengths to build fulfilling relationships and navigate life's challenges with grace and poise.

Libra Compatibility with Other Signs

Libra, the sign represented by the scales, is known for its diplomatic and harmonious nature. People born under this sign are social, charming, and have a strong sense of fairness and justice. When it comes to relationships and compatibility with other signs, Libras tend to seek balance and harmony in their interactions. Let's explore how Libra fares with each of the other zodiac signs:

1. Aries (March 21 - April 19):
Libra and Aries can have a dynamic relationship as they both value independence and have strong personalities. However, conflicts may arise due to their differing approaches to decision-making. Aries is impulsive and decisive, while Libra prefers to weigh all options before making a choice. Finding a middle ground and respecting each other's viewpoints is key to a successful partnership.

2. Taurus (April 20 - May 20):
Libra and Taurus can complement each other well as they both appreciate beauty and luxury. Taurus brings stability and practicality to the relationship, while Libra adds charm and social grace. However, Taurus's stubbornness and Libra's indecisiveness can lead to disagreements. Communication and compromise are essential for these two signs to thrive together.

3. Gemini (May 21 - June 20):

Libra and Gemini share a love for communication and intellectual stimulation. They can engage in deep conversations and enjoy each other's company. Both signs are social and outgoing, making for a lively and engaging relationship. However, Libra's desire for harmony may clash with Gemini's occasional fickleness. Finding ways to address conflicts constructively will strengthen their bond.

4. Cancer (June 21 - July 22):

Libra and Cancer have contrasting emotional needs and communication styles. Cancer values security and emotional connection, while Libra seeks intellectual stimulation and social interaction. Libra's rational approach may clash with Cancer's emotional sensitivity, leading to misunderstandings. Building trust and understanding each other's emotional cues is crucial for these two signs to navigate their differences.

5. Leo (July 23 - August 22):

Libra and Leo share a love for romance, creativity, and luxury. Both signs enjoy being the center of attention and have a flair for drama. While their shared passion for life can create a vibrant relationship, conflicts may arise due to their strong personalities. Libra's diplomatic nature can help smooth over any disagreements, while Leo's generosity and warmth can bring joy to their partnership.

6. Virgo (August 23 - September 22):

Libra and Virgo have complementary qualities that can make for a harmonious partnership. Virgo's practicality and attention to detail balance out Libra's indecisiveness and idealism. Both signs value order and organization, creating a stable and supportive environment. However, Virgo's critical nature may sometimes clash with Libra's desire for harmony. Open communication and mutual respect are vital for these signs to thrive together.

7. Scorpio (October 23 - November 21):

Libra and Scorpio have contrasting approaches to relationships and emotional expression. Scorpio is intense, passionate, and deeply emotional, while Libra is diplomatic, rational, and seeks harmony. Their differences can either create a dynamic and transformative relationship or lead to power struggles and misunderstandings. Trust, honesty, and mutual respect are essential for these signs to navigate their differences and build a strong connection.

8. Sagittarius (November 22 - December 21):

Libra and Sagittarius share a love for adventure, freedom, and intellectual pursuits. Both signs are social, optimistic, and enjoy exploring new ideas and experiences. Their shared zest for life can create a dynamic and exciting relationship. However, Sagittarius's blunt honesty may sometimes clash with Libra's desire to avoid conflict. Finding common ground and respecting each other's differences will strengthen their bond.

9. Capricorn (December 22 - January 19):

Libra and Capricorn approach life with different priorities and values. Capricorn is practical, disciplined, and focused on achieving long-term goals, while Libra is sociable, artistic, and seeks harmony in relationships. Balancing their differing needs for security and social interaction is key to a successful partnership. Capricorn can provide stability and structure, while Libra adds charm and grace to their relationship.

10. Aquarius (January 20 - February 18):

Libra and Aquarius share a love for intellectual pursuits, social causes, and innovation. Both signs value freedom, individuality, and progressive ideas. Their shared vision for a better future can create a dynamic and inspiring relationship. However, Aquarius's aloofness and Libra's indecisiveness may lead to misunderstandings. Embracing each other's unique qualities and communicating openly will strengthen their bond.

11. Pisces (February 19 - March 20):

Libra and Pisces are both compassionate, artistic, and sensitive souls who value harmony and emotional connection. They share a deep empathy for others and a love for creativity and spirituality. Their intuitive nature can create a strong emotional bond and a supportive partnership. However, Libra's rationality and Pisces's emotional depth may sometimes lead to misunderstandings. Building trust and nurturing their emotional connection is essential for these signs to thrive together.

In conclusion, Libra's compatibility with other signs varies based on how well they can navigate their differences, communicate effectively, and find common ground. Building trust, respect, and understanding in relationships is key for Libra to create harmonious and fulfilling connections with a diverse range of personalities across the zodiac.

Famous Libra Personalities

Libras are known for their charm, diplomacy, and love for beauty and balance. People born under the sign of Libra are often admired for their grace, intelligence, and ability to see both sides of a situation. As a result, many famous individuals throughout history have been Libras, making significant contributions to various fields. Here are some notable Libra personalities:

1. Mahatma Gandhi: Known for his nonviolent resistance and leadership in the Indian independence movement, Mahatma Gandhi was born on October 2, 1869. His commitment to peace, justice, and equality has inspired people around the world.

2. Serena Williams: A powerhouse in the world of tennis, Serena Williams, born on September 26, 1981, has achieved numerous Grand Slam titles and is considered one of the greatest athletes of all time. Her determination and skill have made her a role model for aspiring athletes.

3. Will Smith: A versatile actor, rapper, and producer, Will Smith, born on September 25, 1968, has found success in both music and film. Known for his charisma and talent, he has starred in blockbuster movies and received critical acclaim for his performances.

4. Kim Kardashian West: A prominent figure in reality television and business, Kim Kardashian West, born on October 21, 1980, has built a successful empire with her family's show "Keeping Up with the Kardashians" and various business ventures. Her influence in pop culture is undeniable.

5. Oscar Wilde: A renowned playwright, poet, and author, Oscar Wilde, born on October 16, 1854, is celebrated for his wit, humor, and social commentary. His works, such as "The Picture of Dorian Gray" and "The Importance of Being Earnest," continue to be studied and appreciated.

6. Bruno Mars: A talented singer, songwriter, and performer, Bruno Mars, born on October 8, 1985, has captivated audiences with his soulful voice and dynamic stage presence. His chart-topping hits and electrifying performances have earned him multiple Grammy Awards.

7. Gwen Stefani: An iconic singer, fashion designer, and actress, Gwen Stefani, born on October 3, 1969, rose to fame as the lead vocalist of the band No

Doubt before establishing a successful solo career. Her distinctive style and music have made her a pop culture icon.

8. John Lennon: A legendary musician and peace activist, John Lennon, born on October 9, 1940, was a founding member of The Beatles and a prolific songwriter. His music continues to resonate with audiences worldwide, promoting messages of love and unity.

These famous Libra personalities embody the qualities of their zodiac sign, showcasing traits such as creativity, diplomacy, and a strong sense of justice. Their contributions to various fields have left a lasting impact on society, inspiring others to strive for excellence and balance in their own lives.

Chapter 9

Scorpio

Scorpio Overview and Symbolism

Scorpio is the eighth sign of the zodiac, known for its intense and passionate nature. Individuals born under the Scorpio sign are often described as mysterious, powerful, and determined. Symbolized by the scorpion, Scorpios are associated with traits such as loyalty, resourcefulness, and emotional depth.

One of the key characteristics of Scorpios is their intense emotions. They feel things deeply and are not afraid to confront their innermost fears and desires. This emotional depth gives Scorpios a strong sense of intuition and insight into the motivations of others. They are known for their ability to see beneath the surface and uncover hidden truths.

Scorpios are also known for their passionate nature. When they set their sights on a goal or a person, they pursue it with unwavering determination. This intensity can sometimes be perceived as intimidating by others, but it is this drive that allows Scorpios to achieve great success in their endeavors.

Another hallmark trait of Scorpios is their loyalty. Once a Scorpio forms a bond with someone, they are fiercely devoted and protective. They value trust and honesty in their relationships and expect the same level of commitment from others.

In astrology, Scorpio is ruled by the planet Pluto, which symbolizes transformation and rebirth. This influence gives Scorpios a deep sense of introspection and a willingness to confront their own shadows. They are not afraid of change or upheaval, as they understand that true growth often comes from facing challenges head-on.

The element associated with Scorpio is water, which represents emotions and intuition. Scorpios are highly attuned to their feelings and the feelings of those around them. This emotional sensitivity can make them empathetic and compassionate individuals, but it can also lead to moments of intense vulnerability.

Scorpio is a fixed sign, which means that individuals born under this sign are known for their unwavering determination and strong willpower. Once a Scorpio sets their mind to something, they will stop at nothing to achieve it. This resilience and tenacity make Scorpios natural leaders and problem solvers.

Overall, Scorpios are complex and enigmatic individuals who possess a unique blend of passion, loyalty, and intensity. Their ability to delve deep into their emotions and confront challenges head-on sets them apart from others in the zodiac. Whether in love, career, or personal growth, Scorpios approach life with a sense of purpose and a desire for transformation.

Personality Traits of Scorpio

Scorpio, the eighth sign of the zodiac, is represented by the scorpion, a symbol of intensity, passion, and transformation. Those born under the sign of Scorpio are known for their deep and complex personalities, often exhibiting traits that set them apart from others.

One of the key personality traits of Scorpios is their intense and magnetic presence. They possess a powerful aura that draws others towards them, making them natural leaders and influencers. Scorpios are known for their strong willpower and determination, which allows them to pursue their goals with unwavering focus and dedication. They are not afraid to delve into the depths of their emotions and psyche, making them highly intuitive and perceptive individuals.

Scorpios are also known for their passionate nature. They approach life with a fiery intensity and are not afraid to confront challenges head-on. This passion extends to their relationships as well, as Scorpios are fiercely loyal and protective of their loved ones. However, their intensity can sometimes manifest as possessiveness or jealousy, as Scorpios are known to be quite possessive of those they care about.

Another notable trait of Scorpios is their innate desire for transformation and growth. They are constantly seeking to evolve and improve themselves, both personally and spiritually. Scorpios are not content with stagnant situations and are always looking for ways to reinvent themselves and their surroundings. This drive for transformation makes them adept at navigating change and adapting to new circumstances with ease.

Scorpios are also known for their keen intelligence and analytical mindset. They have a natural curiosity and a thirst for knowledge, which drives them to delve deep into complex subjects and uncover hidden truths. Scorpios are skilled at uncovering secrets and mysteries, making them excellent detectives and researchers. Their sharp intuition and perceptive nature allow them to see beyond the surface and understand the underlying motivations and dynamics at play.

On the flip side, Scorpios can also exhibit negative traits such as being secretive and manipulative. Due to their intense nature, Scorpios can sometimes be guarded and secretive about their thoughts and feelings, leading to misunderstandings with others. They can also be prone to manipulation and power struggles, as they are not afraid to use their influence to achieve their goals.

In conclusion, Scorpios are complex and multi-faceted individuals who possess a unique blend of intensity, passion, and depth. Their magnetic presence, passionate nature, desire for transformation, intelligence, and intuitive abilities set them apart from other zodiac signs. While they may exhibit some negative traits such as secrecy and manipulation, Scorpios are ultimately driven by a deep desire for growth and self-discovery, making them powerful and transformative forces in the world.

Scorpio in Love and Relationships

Scorpio, the enigmatic and intense water sign of the zodiac, is known for their passionate and deep connections in love and relationships. When a Scorpio falls in love, they do so with unwavering devotion and loyalty, making them one of the most intense and committed partners in the zodiac.

Scorpios are drawn to deep emotional connections and are not afraid to delve into the depths of their own and their partner's feelings. They are highly intuitive and can sense the emotions and needs of their partner without them having to say a word. This intuitive nature allows Scorpios to create a strong emotional bond with their partners, fostering a sense of trust and intimacy that is unparalleled.

In relationships, Scorpios are known for their intense and passionate nature. They crave a deep and meaningful connection with their partner and are not satisfied with superficial or casual relationships. Scorpios are fiercely loyal and protective of their loved ones, willing to go to great lengths to ensure their partner's happiness and well-being.

However, Scorpios can also be possessive and jealous in relationships. Their intense emotions and desire for control can sometimes lead them to be overly possessive of their partner, causing tension and conflicts in the relationship. It is important for Scorpios to learn to trust their partner and not let their insecurities and fears dictate their actions.

In love, Scorpios are known for their magnetic attraction and seductive charm. They exude a mysterious aura that draws others towards them, making them irresistible to many. Scorpios are not afraid to express their desires and are passionate lovers who are willing to explore the depths of intimacy with their partner.

When it comes to compatibility, Scorpios are most compatible with Cancer, Pisces, and other Scorpios. These signs share a deep emotional bond with Scorpio and understand their intense nature, creating a harmonious and fulfilling relationship. Scorpios also do well with earth signs like Taurus and Capricorn, who can provide stability and grounding to the intense Scorpio energy.

In conclusion, Scorpios are intense and passionate individuals when it comes to love and relationships. They seek deep emotional connections and are willing to invest themselves fully in their relationships. While Scorpios can be possessive and jealous at times, their loyalty and devotion make them exceptional partners for those who are willing to dive into the depths of their emotions with them.

Career and Ambitions of Scorpio

Scorpios are known for their intense and passionate nature, which also translates into their career pursuits and ambitions. Individuals born under the Scorpio zodiac sign are driven, determined, and highly focused on achieving their goals. They are natural leaders who possess a strong sense of ambition and a desire for success in all their endeavors.

Career Paths: Scorpios are drawn to careers that allow them to delve deep into complex and challenging situations. They excel in fields that require strategic thinking, problem-solving skills, and a keen analytical mind. Some common career paths that align with Scorpio's strengths include psychology, research, investigative journalism, law enforcement, and the sciences. They are also well-suited for careers in finance, business management, and entrepreneurship, where their strong intuition and ability to navigate through uncertainties can lead to success.

Ambitions: Scorpios are ambitious individuals who are not afraid to set high goals for themselves and work tirelessly to achieve them. They have a deep sense of purpose and are driven by a desire to make a meaningful impact in their chosen field. Scorpios are not satisfied with mediocrity; they strive for excellence and are willing to put in the hard work and dedication required to reach the top of their profession.

Leadership Qualities: Scorpios possess natural leadership qualities that make them stand out in any professional setting. They are decisive, assertive, and have a commanding presence that inspires others to follow their lead. Scorpios are not afraid to take risks and make tough decisions when necessary, which often sets them apart as visionary leaders in their respective industries.

Career Challenges: While Scorpios have a strong drive for success, they may also face challenges in their career due to their intense and sometimes controlling nature. Scorpios can be secretive and possessive, which can sometimes create conflicts in the workplace. It is important for Scorpios to work on developing healthy communication skills and learning to trust others to avoid potential power struggles.

Career Growth: Scorpios thrive in environments where they are given autonomy and the freedom to express their creativity and innovation. They are constantly seeking opportunities for growth and advancement in their careers. Scorpios are not afraid to take on new challenges and push themselves outside of their comfort zones to continue evolving and expanding their skills and knowledge.

In conclusion, Scorpios are driven and ambitious individuals who excel in careers that allow them to utilize their analytical skills, leadership qualities, and passionate nature. They are natural strategists who are not afraid to take on challenges and push themselves to achieve their goals. By harnessing their strengths and working on their weaknesses, Scorpios can carve out successful and fulfilling careers that align with their ambitions and aspirations.

Strengths and Weaknesses of Scorpio

Scorpio, the eighth sign of the zodiac, is known for its intensity, passion, and depth. Individuals born under the Scorpio sign are often described as mysterious, determined, and resourceful. In this section, we will delve into the strengths and weaknesses of Scorpio personalities to gain a deeper understanding of their characteristics.

Strengths of Scorpio:

1. Passionate and Intense: Scorpios are known for their intense emotions and passion. They approach life with a deep sense of commitment and are not afraid to go after what they want with fervor.

2. Determined and Focused: Scorpios are highly determined individuals who set their sights on their goals and work tirelessly to achieve them. Their laser-like focus allows them to overcome obstacles and challenges with resilience.

3. Resourceful and Strategic: Scorpios possess a keen sense of resourcefulness and strategic thinking. They are adept at finding creative solutions to problems and are skilled at navigating complex situations with ease.

4. Loyal and Protective: Scorpios are fiercely loyal to their loved ones and are willing to go to great lengths to protect and support them. They form deep bonds with those they care about and are known for their unwavering loyalty.

5. Intuitive and Perceptive: Scorpios have a strong intuition and are highly perceptive individuals. They can often sense underlying emotions and motives, making them adept at understanding the true nature of situations and people.

Weaknesses of Scorpio:

1. Jealous and Possessive: Scorpios can be prone to feelings of jealousy and possessiveness in relationships. Their intense emotions can sometimes lead to controlling behaviors and a need for power and control.

2. Secretive and Distrustful: Scorpios have a tendency to keep their feelings and thoughts guarded, leading to a sense of secrecy and mystery. They can also be distrustful of others, which can create challenges in forming deep and trusting relationships.

3. Vindictive and Resentful: Scorpios have a strong sense of justice and can be unforgiving when they feel wronged. They may hold onto grudges and resentments, which can impact their ability to move forward and let go of past hurts.

4. Manipulative and Intense: Scorpios have a complex nature that can sometimes manifest as manipulative or controlling behavior. Their intensity and strong will can be intimidating to others, leading to power struggles and conflicts.

5. Stubborn and Obsessive: Scorpios can be stubborn and resistant to change, holding onto their beliefs and opinions with unwavering determination. They may also become fixated on certain ideas or goals, leading to obsessive tendencies.

In conclusion, Scorpios possess a unique blend of strengths and weaknesses that shape their personalities and interactions with the world. By understanding these traits, Scorpios can harness their strengths to achieve their goals while working on overcoming their weaknesses to cultivate more harmonious relationships and personal growth.

Scorpio Compatibility with Other Signs

Scorpio, the eighth sign of the zodiac, is known for its intensity, passion, and determination. People born under this sign are often seen as mysterious, powerful, and deeply emotional. When it comes to relationships, Scorpios are known for their loyalty and devotion, but they can also be possessive and jealous at times. Understanding Scorpio's compatibility with other signs can provide valuable insights into how they interact with different personalities.

Scorpio Compatibility with Other Signs:

1. Scorpio and Aries:
Scorpio and Aries share a strong physical attraction and intense chemistry. Both signs are passionate and determined, but they can also be stubborn and demanding. Aries may find Scorpio's intensity overwhelming, while Scorpio may struggle with Aries' impulsiveness. With effort and compromise, these two signs can create a powerful and dynamic relationship.

2. Scorpio and Taurus:
Scorpio and Taurus are both strong-willed and loyal signs, which can create a stable and committed relationship. Taurus provides stability and security, while Scorpio brings depth and intensity to the partnership. However, Taurus may find Scorpio's emotional intensity challenging, while Scorpio may feel that Taurus is too stubborn. Communication and trust are key for this pairing to thrive.

3. Scorpio and Gemini:
Scorpio and Gemini have very different approaches to life and relationships. Scorpio values depth and emotional connection, while Gemini seeks variety and intellectual stimulation. This mismatch can lead to misunderstandings and conflicts. Scorpio may find Gemini superficial, while Gemini may feel suffocated by Scorpio's intensity. Both signs need to work on understanding and respecting each other's differences.

4. Scorpio and Cancer:
Scorpio and Cancer share a deep emotional bond and intuitive understanding of each other's feelings. Both signs are sensitive and nurturing, creating a harmonious and supportive relationship. Cancer provides emotional security and warmth, while Scorpio offers loyalty and protection. This pairing can be very fulfilling and long-lasting if both partners are willing to communicate openly and honestly.

5. Scorpio and Leo:
Scorpio and Leo are both strong-willed and passionate signs, which can lead to power struggles and conflicts. Scorpio may feel threatened by Leo's need

for attention and admiration, while Leo may find Scorpio's intensity overwhelming. However, if both signs can learn to respect each other's strengths and differences, they can create a fiery and dynamic relationship.

6. Scorpio and Virgo:
Scorpio and Virgo share a practical and analytical approach to life, which can create a stable and grounded relationship. Virgo provides Scorpio with stability and support, while Scorpio encourages Virgo to embrace their emotions and passions. Both signs value loyalty and honesty, which can strengthen their bond. Communication and compromise are essential for this pairing to thrive.

7. Scorpio and Libra:
Scorpio and Libra have very different personalities and priorities, which can lead to challenges in their relationship. Scorpio values depth and intensity, while Libra seeks harmony and balance. Scorpio may find Libra indecisive and superficial, while Libra may feel that Scorpio is too intense and controlling. Finding a middle ground and respecting each other's differences is crucial for this pairing to work.

In conclusion, Scorpio's compatibility with other signs varies depending on the individual personalities involved. While some pairings may face challenges due to differences in communication styles and priorities, others can thrive through mutual understanding and respect. By being open to compromise and willing to work through conflicts, Scorpio can build strong and lasting relationships with a wide range of zodiac signs.

Famous Scorpio Personalities
Scorpios are known for their intensity, passion, and determination. People born under this water sign are often mysterious, magnetic, and possess a deep sense of emotional depth. Here are some famous Scorpio personalities who have made a mark in various fields:

1. Ryan Gosling (November 12, 1980) - This Canadian actor is known for his versatile roles in films such as "La La Land," "Drive," and "The Notebook." With his brooding intensity and charismatic presence, Gosling embodies many Scorpio traits in his performances.

2. Julia Roberts (October 28, 1967) - As one of Hollywood's most renowned actresses, Roberts has captivated audiences with her talent and charm. Known for her roles in films like "Pretty Woman" and "Erin Brockovich," she showcases the Scorpio determination and depth in her acting.

3. Leonardo DiCaprio (November 11, 1974) - This Academy Award-winning actor is celebrated for his roles in iconic films like "Titanic," "The Revenant," and "The Wolf of Wall Street." DiCaprio's intense portrayals and commitment to his craft reflect the Scorpio traits of passion and ambition.

4. Katy Perry (October 25, 1984) - As a pop sensation known for hits like "Firework" and "Roar," Perry embodies the Scorpio flair for transformation and reinvention. Her bold performances and emotional depth resonate with her Scorpio sun sign.

5. Pablo Picasso (October 25, 1881) - This legendary artist revolutionized the world of modern art with his innovative style and groundbreaking creations. Picasso's intense creativity and emotional depth reflect the Scorpio penchant for delving into the depths of the soul.

6. Hillary Clinton (October 26, 1947) - As a former First Lady, Secretary of State, and presidential candidate, Clinton embodies the Scorpio traits of resilience, ambition, and tenacity. Her unwavering dedication to public service and political career showcases the Scorpio drive for success.

7. Anne Hathaway (November 12, 1982) - This talented actress has captivated audiences with her performances in films like "Les Misérables," "The Devil Wears Prada," and "The Princess Diaries." Hathaway's emotional range and intensity mirror the Scorpio passion for their craft.

8. Drake (October 24, 1986) - As a Grammy Award-winning rapper and singer, Drake has made a significant impact on the music industry with hits like "Hotline Bling" and "God's Plan." His introspective lyrics and emotional depth resonate with his Scorpio sun sign.

9. Emma Stone (November 6, 1988) - This Academy Award-winning actress is known for her roles in films like "La La Land," "The Help," and "Birdman." Stone's versatility, depth, and emotional range showcase the Scorpio traits of intensity and passion.

10. Ezra Miller (September 30, 1992) - This talented actor has gained acclaim for his roles in films like "Fantastic Beasts and Where to Find Them" and "The Perks of Being a Wallflower." Miller's unique approach to acting and transformative performances embody the Scorpio spirit of depth and complexity.

These famous Scorpio personalities exemplify the traits and qualities associated with this enigmatic and intense zodiac sign. From the world of entertainment to politics and art, Scorpios leave a lasting impact with their passion, determination, and emotional depth.

Chapter 10

Sagittarius

Sagittarius Overview and Symbolism

Sagittarius, the ninth sign of the zodiac, is symbolized by the Archer, representing the adventurous and philosophical nature of those born under this sign. People born between November 22 and December 21 fall under the Sagittarius sign, ruled by Jupiter, the planet of expansion, growth, and abundance. Known for their optimistic and free-spirited personality, Sagittarians are always seeking new experiences and opportunities for growth.

Overview and Symbolism:

Sagittarius is associated with traits such as enthusiasm, independence, and a love for adventure. The symbol of the Archer reflects the Sagittarian's aim for higher knowledge and truth. They are natural explorers, both in the physical and intellectual realms, always seeking to expand their horizons and gain a deeper understanding of the world around them.

Personality Traits of Sagittarius:

Sagittarians are known for their outgoing and friendly nature. They have a positive outlook on life and are always ready for new challenges. Their adventurous spirit often leads them to travel and explore different cultures and philosophies. Sagittarians are also known for their honesty and straightforwardness, sometimes to the point of bluntness.

Sagittarius in Love and Relationships:

In relationships, Sagittarians value their freedom and independence. They seek partners who share their love for adventure and are open-minded and intellectually stimulating. While they may struggle with commitment at times, once they find a partner who understands their need for space and growth, Sagittarians can be loyal and passionate companions.

Career and Ambitions of Sagittarius:

Sagittarians thrive in careers that allow them to explore and expand their knowledge. They are natural teachers, philosophers, and adventurers, excelling in fields such as education, travel, publishing, and philosophy. Sagittarians are motivated by the pursuit of truth and meaning, and they are always looking for opportunities to grow and evolve in their professional lives.

Strengths and Weaknesses of Sagittarius:
The strengths of Sagittarians lie in their optimism, enthusiasm, and adaptability. They are natural leaders who inspire others with their vision and charisma. However, Sagittarians can also be impatient, restless, and prone to taking risks without considering the consequences. Their blunt honesty can sometimes come across as tactless or insensitive.

Sagittarius Compatibility with Other Signs:
Sagittarians are most compatible with fellow fire signs Aries and Leo, as well as air signs Gemini and Aquarius. Their adventurous spirit and love for intellectual pursuits make them a good match for these signs. Sagittarians may struggle in relationships with earth signs Taurus, Virgo, and Capricorn, who may find their spontaneity and lack of routine challenging.

Famous Sagittarius Personalities:
Some famous Sagittarians include Walt Disney, Taylor Swift, Brad Pitt, and Jay-Z, all of whom embody the adventurous and optimistic qualities of this sign.

In conclusion, Sagittarius is a sign characterized by a thirst for knowledge, adventure, and growth. Those born under this sign are natural explorers who are always seeking to expand their horizons and uncover the deeper truths of life. With their optimism and philosophical nature, Sagittarians inspire others to dream big and embrace the unknown with courage and enthusiasm.

Personality Traits of Sagittarius

Sagittarius, the ninth sign of the zodiac, is known for its optimistic and adventurous nature. People born under this sign, which falls between November 22 and December 21, are often characterized by their love for freedom, exploration, and intellectual pursuits.

One of the key personality traits of Sagittarius individuals is their inherent optimism and positive outlook on life. They tend to see the glass as half full and approach challenges with a sense of enthusiasm and confidence. This optimism allows them to take risks and pursue their goals with a sense of adventure, always seeking new experiences and opportunities for growth.

Sagittarians are also known for their adventurous spirit and love for travel and exploration. They have a deep curiosity about the world around them and are constantly seeking to expand their horizons through new experiences and knowledge. This wanderlust drives them to explore different cultures, philosophies, and belief systems, making them natural seekers of truth and wisdom.

In addition to their adventurous nature, Sagittarians are known for their intellectual curiosity and philosophical mindset. They have a deep interest in understanding the meaning of life and are drawn to subjects like spirituality, religion, and higher education. This intellectual curiosity drives them to seek out new experiences and knowledge, often leading them to pursue careers in fields like teaching, philosophy, or publishing.

Sagittarius individuals are also known for their honesty and straightforwardness. They value authenticity and integrity in their relationships and interactions with others. While their bluntness can sometimes come across as tactless, Sagittarians are known for speaking their minds and being unafraid to express their opinions, even if they are controversial.

On the flip side, Sagittarians can also be prone to restlessness and impatience. Their love for freedom and independence can sometimes lead them to be inconsistent or unreliable in their commitments. They may struggle with routine and may become bored easily if they feel stagnant or constrained in any way.

In relationships, Sagittarians are known for their warmth, generosity, and sense of humor. They value honesty and open communication in their partnerships and are always looking for a partner who shares their sense of adventure and love for exploration. While they may struggle with commitment at times, Sagittarians are loyal and devoted to those they care about.

Overall, Sagittarius individuals are characterized by their optimistic outlook, adventurous spirit, intellectual curiosity, honesty, and warmth. Their love for exploration and pursuit of knowledge make them natural seekers of truth and wisdom, always striving to expand their horizons and grow as individuals.

Sagittarius in Love and Relationships

Sagittarius, the ninth sign of the zodiac, is known for its adventurous and free-spirited nature. In love and relationships, Sagittarians are passionate and optimistic individuals who seek excitement, growth, and intellectual stimulation.

When it comes to love, Sagittarians are independent and value their freedom. They are not the type to be tied down or constrained by traditional relationship norms. Instead, they thrive in relationships that allow them the space to explore and experience new things. Sagittarians are always seeking to expand their horizons, both mentally and physically, and they look for a partner who shares their thirst for knowledge and adventure.

In a romantic relationship, Sagittarians are loyal and honest partners. They are known for their straightforward communication style and appreciate the same level of honesty in return. Sagittarians value open communication and intellectual conversations with their partners, and they are attracted to individuals who can engage them in meaningful discussions and debates.

Sagittarians are also known for their optimism and positivity, which can be infectious in a relationship. They have a natural ability to see the silver lining in any situation and can uplift their partners during challenging times. Their adventurous spirit and love for exploration can bring a sense of excitement and spontaneity to the relationship, keeping things fresh and dynamic.

However, Sagittarians can be prone to restlessness and a fear of commitment. They may struggle with settling down or feeling tied down in a long-term relationship. It is important for their partners to give them the space they need to pursue their interests and maintain their independence while also providing emotional support and stability.

In terms of compatibility, Sagittarians are most compatible with fellow fire signs Aries and Leo, as well as air signs Gemini and Aquarius. These signs share Sagittarius' love for adventure, freedom, and intellectual pursuits, creating a harmonious and dynamic relationship.

On the other hand, Sagittarians may clash with water signs Cancer, Scorpio, and Pisces, as well as earth signs Taurus, Virgo, and Capricorn. These signs may find Sagittarius' restless nature and need for independence challenging in a relationship.

In conclusion, Sagittarius individuals bring a sense of excitement, passion, and optimism to their relationships. They value honesty, communication, and intellectual stimulation in a partner, and thrive in relationships that allow them the freedom to explore and grow. By understanding and appreciating a Sagittarius' unique qualities and needs, partners can build a strong and fulfilling relationship with these adventurous and spirited individuals.

Career and Ambitions of Sagittarius

Sagittarius, the Explorer, is known for their adventurous and optimistic nature, which also reflects in their career choices and ambitions. Individuals born under the sign of Sagittarius are driven by a strong sense of curiosity and a desire for new experiences, making them well-suited for careers that involve travel, exploration, and learning.

Career Paths and Ambitions:

Sagittarians are natural explorers and are often drawn to careers that allow them to expand their horizons and seek out new challenges. They are highly adaptable and thrive in dynamic environments where they can continuously learn and grow. Some common career paths that align with the ambitions of Sagittarius include:

1. Travel Industry: Sagittarians have a deep love for travel and adventure, making them well-suited for careers in the travel industry such as travel writer, tour guide, or travel photographer. They enjoy exploring new cultures and sharing their experiences with others.

2. Education and Academia: Sagittarians have a thirst for knowledge and a passion for learning, making them excellent educators, professors, or researchers. They enjoy sharing their wisdom and insights with others and are often drawn to fields such as philosophy, religion, or higher education.

3. Entrepreneurship: Sagittarians are known for their independent spirit and innovative ideas, making them natural entrepreneurs. They are not afraid to take risks and are always seeking new opportunities for growth and expansion. Sagittarians may excel in starting their own business or pursuing ventures that align with their values and passions.

4. Media and Publishing: Sagittarians are gifted communicators and may find success in careers that involve writing, broadcasting, or public speaking. They have a knack for storytelling and are able to captivate audiences with their charisma and enthusiasm. Careers in journalism, publishing, or broadcasting may appeal to Sagittarians.

5. Legal and Justice System: Sagittarians are known for their strong sense of justice and fairness, making them well-suited for careers in law or the justice system. They have a natural ability to see both sides of an argument and are skilled at resolving conflicts and finding solutions. Sagittarians may excel as lawyers, judges, or legal advocates.

Overall, Sagittarians are driven by a sense of purpose and a desire to make a positive impact on the world around them. They are ambitious individuals who are not afraid to take risks and pursue their dreams with passion and determination. By following their instincts and staying true to their values, Sagittarians can achieve success and fulfillment in their chosen careers.

Strengths and Weaknesses of Sagittarius

Sagittarius, the adventurous and optimistic fire sign of the zodiac, is known for its enthusiastic and philosophical nature. Individuals born under the sign of Sagittarius, typically between November 22 and December 21, possess a unique set of strengths and weaknesses that shape their personality and interactions with the world.

Strengths of Sagittarius:

1. Optimistic and Enthusiastic: Sagittarians are known for their boundless optimism and enthusiasm. They have a positive outlook on life and are always ready to embrace new experiences with open arms.

2. Adventurous and Independent: Sagittarians have a deep-seated wanderlust and a strong desire for freedom. They thrive on exploring new territories, both physically and intellectually, and are not afraid to take risks in pursuit of their passions.

3. Philosophical and Intellectual: Sagittarians have a keen interest in exploring the deeper meanings of life. They are naturally philosophical and enjoy engaging in discussions about spirituality, ethics, and the bigger questions of existence.

4. Honest and Straightforward: Individuals born under the sign of Sagittarius are known for their honesty and straightforwardness. They value authenticity and have a strong moral compass, which guides their interactions with others.

5. Generous and Optimistic: Sagittarians are generous souls who enjoy helping others and spreading positivity wherever they go. Their natural warmth and kindness make them popular among friends and loved ones.

Weaknesses of Sagittarius:

1. Impulsive and Restless: Sagittarians can sometimes be impulsive and restless, always seeking the next thrill or adventure. This can lead to a lack of focus and commitment in certain areas of their lives.

2. Tactless and Blunt: Due to their honesty and straightforwardness, Sagittarians may come across as tactless or blunt at times. They value truth over diplomacy, which can sometimes hurt the feelings of more sensitive individuals.

3. Overconfident and Self-Righteous: Sagittarians have a tendency to be overly confident in their beliefs and opinions. This can sometimes lead to a sense of self-righteousness and a lack of consideration for the perspectives of others.

4. Commitment Issues: Sagittarians value their freedom and independence above all else, which can make them hesitant to commit to long-term relationships or responsibilities. They may struggle with staying grounded and focused on one path for an extended period.

5. Restlessness and Impatience: Sagittarians are known for their restless nature and dislike of routine. They may become impatient with mundane tasks or situations that do not stimulate their adventurous spirit, leading to a lack of follow-through on certain projects.

Overall, Sagittarians are vibrant and dynamic individuals with a zest for life and a passion for exploration. By embracing their strengths and working on their weaknesses, they can unlock their full potential and lead fulfilling lives filled with adventure, growth, and wisdom.

Sagittarius Compatibility with Other Signs

Sagittarius is known for their adventurous and optimistic nature, making them a lively and engaging partner in relationships. Understanding how Sagittarius interacts with other zodiac signs can give us valuable insights into the dynamics of their compatibility.

Sagittarius and Aries: Both Fire signs, Sagittarius and Aries share a passionate and energetic approach to life. They inspire each other and enjoy engaging in new experiences together. Their relationship is dynamic and exciting, filled with shared adventures and a mutual understanding of each other's need for independence.

Sagittarius and Taurus: Sagittarius and Taurus have different approaches to life, with Sagittarius being more spontaneous and Taurus being more grounded and practical. While they may have some challenges in understanding each other's perspectives, they can complement each other well if they are willing to communicate and compromise.

Sagittarius and Gemini: Both Sagittarius and Gemini are Air signs, which means they share a love for intellectual stimulation and communication. They have a natural understanding of each other's thoughts and ideas, making their relationship intellectually stimulating and full of lively discussions.

Sagittarius and Cancer: Sagittarius and Cancer have different emotional needs and approaches to relationships. Sagittarius values freedom and independence, while Cancer values security and emotional connection. They may need to work on understanding and respecting each other's differences to make their relationship work.

Sagittarius and Leo: Sagittarius and Leo are both Fire signs, which means they share a strong passion for life and a desire for excitement. They understand each other's need for adventure and fun, making their relationship dynamic and full of energy. Both signs encourage each other to pursue their goals and dreams.

Sagittarius and Virgo: Sagittarius and Virgo have different approaches to life, with Sagittarius being more spontaneous and Virgo being more practical and detail-oriented. They may need to work on understanding and appreciating each other's differences to find a balance in their relationship.

Sagittarius and Libra: Sagittarius and Libra share a love for beauty, harmony, and socializing. They enjoy engaging in intellectual conversations and exploring new ideas together. Their relationship is characterized by mutual respect and understanding, making them compatible partners.

Sagittarius and Scorpio: Sagittarius and Scorpio have different emotional needs and approaches to relationships. Sagittarius values freedom and independence, while Scorpio values intensity and emotional depth. They may need to work on understanding and accepting each other's differences to build a strong and lasting connection.

Sagittarius and Capricorn: Sagittarius and Capricorn have different approaches to life, with Sagittarius being more adventurous and Capricorn being more practical and goal-oriented. They may need to find a balance between Sagittarius's need for freedom and Capricorn's need for stability to make their relationship work.

Sagittarius and Aquarius: Sagittarius and Aquarius share a love for independence, freedom, and intellectual stimulation. They understand each other's need for space and individuality, making their relationship harmonious and supportive. They enjoy engaging in deep conversations and exploring new ideas together.

Sagittarius and Pisces: Sagittarius and Pisces have different emotional needs and approaches to relationships. Sagittarius values honesty and directness, while Pisces values sensitivity and emotional connection. They may need to work on understanding and respecting each other's differences to build a strong and lasting bond.

In conclusion, Sagittarius is compatible with a variety of zodiac signs, each offering unique qualities and dynamics to the relationship. By understanding and appreciating the differences and similarities between Sagittarius and their partner's zodiac signs, individuals can navigate their relationships with more awareness and understanding.

Famous Sagittarius Personalities

Sagittarius, the ninth sign of the zodiac, is known for its adventurous and optimistic nature. Those born under this sign are often characterized by their love for freedom, exploration, and philosophical pursuits. Famous Sagittarius personalities embody these traits and have made significant contributions in various fields. Let's delve into some of the most notable Sagittarius individuals:

1. Walt Disney (December 5, 1901) - The visionary behind the iconic Disney empire, Walt Disney was a Sagittarius known for his creativity, innovation, and imagination. His pioneering work in animation and entertainment continues to inspire generations worldwide.

2. Taylor Swift (December 13, 1989) - A talented singer-songwriter, Taylor Swift is a Sagittarius known for her storytelling lyrics and chart-topping hits. Her success in the music industry reflects the Sagittarian traits of passion, determination, and optimism.

3. Bruce Lee (November 27, 1940) - The legendary martial artist and actor, Bruce Lee, was a Sagittarius known for his physical prowess, discipline, and philosophical insights. His influence on martial arts and popular culture is a testament to the adventurous spirit of Sagittarius.

4. Jay-Z (December 4, 1969) - A successful rapper, entrepreneur, and philanthropist, Jay-Z is a Sagittarius known for his business acumen, creativity, and resilience. His career achievements exemplify the Sagittarian traits of ambition, confidence, and adaptability.

5. Steven Spielberg (December 18, 1946) - The acclaimed filmmaker Steven Spielberg is a Sagittarius known for his visionary storytelling and cinematic mastery. His contributions to the film industry showcase the Sagittarian traits of exploration, creativity, and passion.

6. Britney Spears (December 2, 1981) - A pop icon and performer, Britney Spears is a Sagittarius known for her musical talent, charisma, and stage presence. Her enduring impact on the music industry reflects the Sagittarian traits of enthusiasm, optimism, and expressiveness.

7. Winston Churchill (November 30, 1874) - The revered British statesman Winston Churchill was a Sagittarius known for his leadership, courage, and eloquence. His role in shaping history during World War II exemplifies the Sagittarian traits of determination, wisdom, and resilience.

8. Samuel L. Jackson (December 21, 1948) - A versatile actor known for his powerful performances, Samuel L. Jackson is a Sagittarius celebrated for his talent, charisma, and versatility. His iconic roles in film and television showcase the Sagittarian traits of passion, confidence, and independence.

9. Tina Turner (November 26, 1939) - The legendary singer and performer Tina Turner is a Sagittarius known for her electrifying stage presence, soulful voice, and resilience. Her music career embodies the Sagittarian traits of passion, freedom, and authenticity.

10. Brad Pitt (December 18, 1963) - A renowned actor and producer, Brad Pitt is a Sagittarius known for his talent, charisma, and versatility. His success in Hollywood reflects the Sagittarian traits of enthusiasm, creativity, and adaptability.

These famous Sagittarius personalities demonstrate the diverse talents and qualities associated with this adventurous and optimistic zodiac sign. Their achievements serve as inspiration for all Sagittarians to embrace their unique strengths and pursue their passions with courage and determination.

Chapter 11

Capricorn

Capricorn Overview and Symbolism

Capricorn is the tenth sign of the zodiac, represented by the symbol of the Goat. Individuals born under this sign, which spans from December 22 to January 19, are known for their ambitious and disciplined nature. Capricorns are ruled by the planet Saturn, the planet of discipline, responsibility, and structure. This influence gives Capricorns their reputation for being hardworking, practical, and goal-oriented.

Symbolism of Capricorn:

The symbol of the Goat in Capricorn represents resilience, determination, and the ability to climb to great heights. Just like the mountain goat that steadily navigates steep terrain, Capricorns are known for their perseverance and ability to overcome obstacles in pursuit of their goals. The symbol also embodies the idea of reaching the pinnacle of success through hard work and dedication.

Personality Traits of Capricorn:

Capricorns are known for their practicality, ambition, and strong work ethic. They are reliable, responsible, and disciplined individuals who approach life with a sense of purpose. Capricorns are often seen as mature beyond their years, with a keen sense of responsibility and a focus on long-term goals. They are strategic thinkers who excel at planning and executing their plans with precision.

Capricorn in Love and Relationships:

In relationships, Capricorns are loyal, committed, and dependable partners. They value stability and security in their relationships and are willing to put in the effort to make them work. While they may come off as reserved or cautious initially, Capricorns are deeply caring and attentive to their loved ones. They seek a partner who shares their values and is equally dedicated to building a strong foundation for the future.

Career and Ambitions of Capricorn:
Capricorns excel in careers that require focus, determination, and hard work. They are natural leaders and excel in positions of authority where they can demonstrate their organizational skills and strategic thinking. Capricorns are drawn to professions that offer stability and opportunities for advancement, such as business, finance, law, and management. They are willing to put in the effort to climb the corporate ladder and achieve their professional goals.

Strengths and Weaknesses of Capricorn:
Capricorns are known for their determination, practicality, and ambition. They are reliable, responsible, and disciplined individuals who excel in leadership roles. However, their strong focus on work and success can sometimes make them appear cold or detached. Capricorns may also struggle with perfectionism and a tendency to be overly critical of themselves and others. Balancing their ambitious nature with self-care and relaxation is essential for Capricorns to maintain their well-being.

Capricorn Compatibility with Other Signs:
Capricorns are most compatible with Taurus, Virgo, and Pisces. Taurus and Virgo share Capricorn's practical nature and desire for stability, creating a strong foundation for a lasting relationship. Pisces, on the other hand, offers Capricorn emotional depth and understanding, complementing their more pragmatic approach to life.

Famous Capricorn Personalities:
Some famous Capricorns include Michelle Obama, Denzel Washington, Kate Middleton, and Muhammad Ali. These individuals embody the determination, ambition, and success commonly associated with the Capricorn sign.

In conclusion, Capricorn is a sign characterized by ambition, discipline, and a strong work ethic. Individuals born under this sign are driven to achieve their goals, overcome challenges, and build a solid foundation for success. By leveraging their practicality and strategic thinking, Capricorns can reach great heights in both their personal and professional lives.

Personality Traits of Capricorn

Capricorn, the tenth sign of the zodiac, is symbolized by the Sea-Goat, representing the fusion of earth and water elements. Capricorns are known for their ambitious and disciplined nature, as well as their strong work ethic and determination to succeed in all aspects of life.

Personality Traits of Capricorn:

Capricorns are characterized by their practicality, responsibility, and reliability. They are often seen as mature beyond their years, with a natural ability to take charge and lead others. Capricorns are known for their ambition and drive to achieve their goals, making them highly motivated individuals who are willing to put in the hard work necessary to reach their desired outcomes.

One of the key traits of Capricorns is their sense of duty and obligation. They take their responsibilities seriously and are dedicated to fulfilling their commitments, whether in their personal relationships or professional endeavors. Capricorns are highly organized and methodical in their approach to tasks, often excelling in leadership roles where their structured and disciplined nature can shine.

Capricorns are also known for their practicality and pragmatism. They have a keen sense of reality and are adept at making sound decisions based on logic and reason rather than emotions. This grounded approach to life allows Capricorns to navigate challenges with a level-headed perspective, finding practical solutions to complex problems.

In addition to their practicality, Capricorns are also known for their loyalty and dependability. They are steadfast and reliable friends and partners who can be counted on to offer support and guidance when needed. Capricorns value honesty and integrity in their relationships, and they strive to maintain a strong sense of loyalty and commitment to those they care about.

While Capricorns are often seen as serious and reserved individuals, they also have a playful and witty side to their personality. They have a dry sense of humor and enjoy engaging in intellectual conversations with others. Capricorns are highly intelligent and strategic thinkers, able to analyze situations from multiple angles and come up with creative solutions.

Overall, Capricorns embody the qualities of hard work, determination, responsibility, and loyalty. They are driven by a desire to achieve success and are willing to put in the effort required to reach their goals. Capricorns are practical and grounded individuals who excel in leadership roles and are valued for their reliability and integrity in all aspects of life.

Capricorn in Love and Relationships

Capricorn, the ambitious and disciplined earth sign ruled by Saturn, approaches love and relationships with the same level of seriousness and dedication they apply to their professional endeavors. Capricorns are known for their practicality, reliability, and commitment, making them reliable partners in romantic relationships.

When it comes to love, Capricorns are not ones to rush into things. They prefer to take their time to get to know a potential partner and build a strong foundation based on trust and mutual respect. Capricorns value stability and security in relationships, and they are willing to put in the effort to make things work in the long run.

In a romantic relationship, Capricorns are loyal and faithful partners. They are not ones to engage in frivolous flings or casual dating; instead, they seek a deep and meaningful connection with their significant other. Capricorns are traditional in their approach to love and relationships, often valuing commitment and monogamy.

Capricorns can be reserved and cautious when it comes to expressing their emotions. They may have a tough exterior but deep down, they are sensitive and caring individuals who value emotional intimacy with their partners. It may take time for a Capricorn to open up and show their vulnerable side, but once they do, they are incredibly loving and supportive partners.

In a relationship, Capricorns are reliable and responsible. They take their commitments seriously and will go to great lengths to support their partner and ensure the success of the relationship. Capricorns are practical problem-solvers and will work hard to overcome any challenges that may arise in the relationship.

Communication is key in a relationship with a Capricorn. They appreciate honesty, directness, and clear communication from their partner. Capricorns value open and honest conversations where both partners can express their needs and concerns openly.

When it comes to compatibility, Capricorns are most compatible with Taurus, Virgo, and other Capricorns. These earth signs share similar values and priorities, making for a harmonious and stable relationship. Capricorns may also find strong connections with water signs like Scorpio and Pisces, who can provide the emotional depth and sensitivity that Capricorns sometimes struggle to express.

In conclusion, Capricorns approach love and relationships with a practical and serious mindset. They value stability, commitment, and loyalty in their romantic partnerships. While they may appear reserved at first, Capricorns are loving, supportive, and dedicated partners who will work hard to build a lasting and fulfilling relationship.

Career and Ambitions of Capricorn

Capricorn is the tenth sign of the zodiac, represented by the symbol of the Goat. Those born under this sign are known for their ambitious nature, disciplined approach, and strong work ethic. Capricorns are driven by a desire for success and are willing to put in the hard work necessary to achieve their goals. Let's delve deeper into the career and ambitions of Capricorn individuals.

Career Path and Ambitions:
Capricorns are natural-born leaders who excel in positions of authority and responsibility. They are drawn to careers that allow them to showcase their organizational skills, strategic thinking, and ability to work diligently towards long-term goals. Capricorns are often found in roles such as CEOs, managers, executives, and entrepreneurs.

Ambitious and determined, Capricorns set high standards for themselves and are willing to go the extra mile to reach the pinnacle of success in their chosen field. They are not afraid to take on challenges and are known for their perseverance in the face of adversity. Capricorns are strategic planners who carefully map out their career trajectory and take calculated risks to achieve their objectives.

Strengths and Weaknesses:
One of the key strengths of Capricorns in their professional lives is their unwavering commitment to excellence. They are reliable, responsible, and conscientious workers who can be counted on to deliver results. Capricorns are also highly resourceful individuals who can navigate complex situations with ease.

However, Capricorns may sometimes be perceived as overly serious or rigid in their approach to work. They can be perfectionists who set impossibly high standards for themselves and others, leading to feelings of frustration or burnout. Capricorns may also struggle with delegating tasks, as they prefer to have full control over their work environment.

Compatibility with Other Signs:
In the workplace, Capricorns work well with signs that share their dedication to hard work and ambition. Signs such as Taurus, Virgo, and Scorpio can complement Capricorn's work style and contribute to a harmonious professional environment. Capricorns may find challenges working with signs that are more impulsive or lack a strong sense of discipline.

Famous Capricorn Personalities:
Numerous successful individuals share the Capricorn zodiac sign. Some famous Capricorns include Michelle Obama, Dolly Parton, LeBron James, Kate Middleton, and Denzel Washington. These individuals exemplify the qualities of determination, resilience, and ambition that are characteristic of Capricorns.

In conclusion, Capricorns are driven by a strong sense of purpose and a desire to achieve their ambitions. Their dedication, perseverance, and strategic mindset make them well-suited for leadership roles and positions of authority. By harnessing their strengths and addressing their weaknesses, Capricorns can thrive in their careers and make a lasting impact on the world around them.

Strengths and Weaknesses of Capricorn

Capricorn, the tenth sign of the zodiac, is represented by the symbol of the Goat. People born under this sign are known for their ambitious and disciplined nature. In this chapter, we will delve into the strengths and weaknesses of Capricorn individuals.

Strengths:

1. Ambitious: Capricorns are driven by their ambitious nature. They set high goals for themselves and work tirelessly to achieve them. Their determination and perseverance help them succeed in their endeavors.

2. Responsible: Capricorns are known for their sense of responsibility. They take their commitments seriously and always strive to fulfill their duties and obligations. They can be relied upon to get the job done efficiently and effectively.

3. Disciplined: Capricorns have a strong sense of discipline and self-control. They are organized and methodical in their approach to tasks, which helps them stay focused and achieve their goals.

4. Patient: Capricorns possess the virtue of patience. They understand that success takes time and are willing to put in the effort required to reach their desired outcomes. Their patient nature allows them to endure challenges and setbacks without losing sight of their objectives.

5. Practical: Capricorns are grounded and practical individuals. They have a realistic outlook on life and approach situations with a practical mindset. This practicality helps them make sound decisions and navigate through life's complexities.

Weaknesses:

1. Pessimistic: Capricorns have a tendency to be pessimistic at times. Their practical nature can sometimes lean towards a negative outlook, causing them to focus on potential obstacles rather than opportunities. This pessimism can hinder their ability to see the brighter side of things.

2. Stubborn: Capricorns can be quite stubborn and resistant to change. Their strong-willed nature makes it challenging for them to adapt to new circumstances or consider alternative perspectives. This rigidity can lead to conflicts in relationships and hinder personal growth.

3. Overly Serious: Capricorns are often perceived as serious and reserved individuals. While their seriousness can be an asset in certain situations, it can also make them appear aloof or unapproachable to others. Finding a balance between seriousness and light-heartedness is essential for Capricorns to connect with others effectively.

4. Workaholic Tendencies: Capricorns are known for their strong work ethic and dedication to their careers. However, their relentless pursuit of success can sometimes lead to workaholic tendencies. They may prioritize work over personal relationships and neglect self-care, leading to burnout and exhaustion.

5. Distrustful: Capricorns can be cautious and distrustful of others, especially in professional settings. Their reserved nature makes it difficult for them to open up and establish trust easily. Building strong relationships based on mutual trust and understanding can be a challenge for Capricorns.

In conclusion, Capricorns possess a unique blend of strengths and weaknesses that shape their personalities and influence their interactions with the world. By leveraging their strengths and addressing their weaknesses, Capricorns can strive for personal growth and success in various aspects of their lives.

Capricorn Compatibility with Other Signs

Capricorn is an earth sign represented by the Goat, and individuals born under this sign are known for their ambitious, disciplined, and practical nature. They are hardworking and focused on achieving their goals, making them compatible with certain signs while posing challenges with others.

Capricorn Compatibility with Other Signs:

1. Capricorn and Taurus: These two earth signs share similar values of stability, security, and practicality. They both appreciate hard work and are committed to their goals, making them a strong and reliable match. Their shared determination and loyalty create a solid foundation for a long-lasting relationship.

2. Capricorn and Virgo: Both Capricorn and Virgo are grounded and detail-oriented signs that value organization and structure. They have a similar approach to life and work, making them highly compatible partners. Their mutual respect for each other's skills and dedication leads to a harmonious and supportive relationship.

3. Capricorn and Scorpio: Capricorn and Scorpio share a deep emotional intensity and a strong sense of loyalty. While they may have different ways of expressing their emotions, they both value honesty and commitment in a relationship. Their shared ambition and drive can create a powerful and dynamic partnership, but they need to communicate openly to avoid power struggles.

4. Capricorn and Pisces: Capricorn and Pisces may seem like an unlikely pair due to their contrasting personalities. Capricorn is practical and grounded, while Pisces is dreamy and sensitive. However, if they can find a balance between their differences, they can complement each other well. Capricorn can provide stability and structure to Pisces, while Pisces can bring creativity and compassion to Capricorn's life.

5. Capricorn and Cancer: Capricorn and Cancer have different ways of approaching life and emotions, but their differences can complement each other. Capricorn's practicality can balance Cancer's emotional nature, while Cancer's nurturing and caring qualities can soften Capricorn's seriousness. They both value security and stability in a relationship, which can create a strong and supportive bond.

6. Capricorn and Aquarius: Capricorn and Aquarius have contrasting personalities and outlooks on life. Capricorn is traditional and practical, while Aquarius is innovative and unconventional. While these differences can create challenges in their relationship, they can also learn from each other and grow together. Capricorn can provide stability and grounding to Aquarius, while Aquarius can inspire Capricorn to think outside the box.

In conclusion, Capricorn's compatibility with other signs depends on the willingness of both partners to understand and appreciate each other's differences. While Capricorn may face challenges with some signs, they can build strong and fulfilling relationships with compatible partners who share their values and goals. Communication, compromise, and mutual respect are essential for Capricorn to thrive in any relationship, regardless of the zodiac sign of their partner.

Famous Capricorn Personalities

Capricorns are known for their ambition, discipline, and determination. They are hardworking individuals who strive for success and are often seen as natural leaders. In this section, we will explore some famous Capricorn personalities who embody these traits and have made a significant impact in their respective fields.

1. Michelle Obama (Born January 17, 1964) - Former First Lady of the United States, Michelle Obama is a Capricorn known for her intelligence, grace, and advocacy for various social causes. She has been a role model for many, using her platform to promote education, healthy living, and women's rights.

2. Muhammad Ali (Born January 17, 1942) - Widely regarded as one of the greatest boxers of all time, Muhammad Ali was a Capricorn known for his charisma, confidence, and athleticism. His fighting spirit and determination made him a global icon both inside and outside the ring.

3. Kate Middleton (Born January 9, 1982) - The Duchess of Cambridge, Kate Middleton is a Capricorn known for her elegance, poise, and dedication to her royal duties. She has become a fashion icon and a beloved member of the British royal family, embodying the traits of a true Capricorn.

4. Denzel Washington (Born December 28, 1954) - A highly acclaimed actor and director, Denzel Washington is a Capricorn known for his versatility, talent, and charisma on screen. He has won multiple awards for his performances and is respected for his dedication to his craft.

5. Dolly Parton (Born January 19, 1946) - A legendary singer, songwriter, and actress, Dolly Parton is a Capricorn known for her creativity, wit, and philanthropy. She has written numerous hit songs and has used her fame to support various charitable causes, showcasing the compassionate side of Capricorns.

6. Lin-Manuel Miranda (Born January 16, 1980) - A Tony Award-winning composer, lyricist, and actor, Lin-Manuel Miranda is a Capricorn known for his creativity, passion, and innovative work in musical theater. He is the mastermind behind the critically acclaimed musicals "Hamilton" and "In the Heights," showcasing his Capricorn work ethic and talent.

7. Martin Luther King Jr. (Born January 15, 1929) - A prominent civil rights leader and activist, Martin Luther King Jr. was a Capricorn known for his courage, eloquence, and dedication to the fight against racial injustice. His powerful speeches and nonviolent approach to activism have left a lasting impact on society.

8. Bradley Cooper (Born January 5, 1975) - A versatile actor, director, and producer, Bradley Cooper is a Capricorn known for his talent, charm, and determination in the entertainment industry. He has received critical acclaim for his performances and has proven himself as a multifaceted artist.

These famous Capricorn personalities exemplify the traits of their zodiac sign, showcasing qualities such as ambition, hard work, discipline, and success. They serve as inspirations for others to strive for their goals and make a positive impact in their chosen fields, embodying the true spirit of Capricorn.

Chapter 12

Aquarius

Aquarius Overview and Symbolism

Aquarius is the eleventh sign of the zodiac, represented by the Water Bearer. People born under this sign are known for their progressive and innovative nature. They are often seen as visionaries, thinkers, and humanitarians who strive for a better world for all. Aquarians are ruled by the planet Uranus, which is associated with change, originality, and rebellion.

Symbolism of Aquarius:
The symbol for Aquarius is the Water Bearer, pouring water from a jug. This symbolizes the flow of knowledge and wisdom that Aquarians bring to the world. It also represents their desire to bring about positive change and enlightenment to society.

Aquarius is an Air sign, which reflects their intellectual and communicative nature. Aquarians are known for their analytical minds, curiosity, and ability to think outside the box. They are often drawn to new ideas, technology, and social causes that promote equality and justice.

Personality Traits of Aquarius:
Aquarians are known for their independent and unconventional nature. They value their freedom and individuality above all else. They are open-minded, forward-thinking, and unafraid to challenge the status quo. Aquarians are often described as eccentric, quirky, and unpredictable, with a strong sense of idealism and a deep concern for the welfare of others.

In Love and Relationships:
In relationships, Aquarians are loyal and supportive partners who value intellectual connection and shared values. They may seem detached at times due to their independent nature, but they are deeply caring and compassionate individuals. Aquarians are attracted to partners who respect their need for freedom and intellectual stimulation.

Career and Ambitions of Aquarius:
Aquarians excel in careers that allow them to express their creativity, intellect, and originality. They are drawn to fields such as science, technology, humanitarian work, and social activism. Aquarians thrive in environments that value innovation, teamwork, and diversity.

Strengths and Weaknesses of Aquarius:
Aquarians are known for their inventiveness, humanitarianism, and ability to see the big picture. They are natural leaders who inspire others with their vision and passion. However, Aquarians can also be aloof, rebellious, and emotionally detached at times. They may struggle with expressing their emotions and forming deep emotional connections.

Compatibility with Other Signs:
Aquarians are most compatible with fellow Air signs (Gemini and Libra) and Fire signs (Aries, Leo, Sagittarius). They are drawn to partners who share their intellectual curiosity, sense of adventure, and progressive values. Aquarians may have challenges in relationships with more traditional or emotionally intense signs like Taurus or Scorpio.

Famous Aquarius Personalities:
Some famous Aquarians include Oprah Winfrey, Ellen DeGeneres, Abraham Lincoln, and Jennifer Aniston. These individuals embody the visionary and humanitarian qualities of Aquarius, using their influence and creativity to make a positive impact on the world.

Overall, Aquarius is a sign that embodies innovation, progress, and humanitarianism. Those born under this sign are known for their independent spirit, intellectual curiosity, and desire to make a difference in the world.

Personality Traits of Aquarius
Aquarius, the eleventh sign of the zodiac, is represented by the Water Bearer. People born under the Aquarius sign are known for their unique and unconventional approach to life. They are often seen as visionaries, independent thinkers, and humanitarians. Let's delve deeper into the personality traits of Aquarius individuals.

1. Individuality: Aquarians are known for their strong sense of individuality. They value their independence and freedom above all else. They are not afraid to go against the grain and march to the beat of their own drum. Aquarians are often seen as trendsetters and innovators who bring fresh and original ideas to the table.

2. Intellectual: Aquarians have a keen intellect and are natural problem solvers. They approach challenges with a logical and analytical mind, always seeking innovative solutions. They are curious and open-minded, always eager to learn new things and expand their knowledge.

3. Humanitarian: One of the key traits of Aquarius is their deep sense of compassion and concern for the well-being of others. They are often involved in humanitarian causes and strive to make the world a better place for everyone. Aquarians are known for their progressive and forward-thinking attitudes towards social issues.

4. Friendliness: Aquarians are friendly and sociable individuals who enjoy connecting with people from all walks of life. They value their friendships and are always there for their loved ones when needed. Aquarians are good listeners and offer sound advice and support to those around them.

5. Rebellious: Aquarians have a rebellious streak and are not afraid to challenge authority or question the status quo. They are natural non-conformists who push boundaries and seek to break free from traditional norms and expectations.

6. Detached: Despite their friendly and sociable nature, Aquarians can sometimes come across as emotionally detached. They have a tendency to keep their emotions in check and may seem aloof or distant at times. However, this does not mean they lack empathy or care for others.

7. Unpredictable: Aquarians are known for their unpredictability and spontaneity. They thrive on change and excitement, always seeking new experiences and adventures. Their free-spirited nature can sometimes lead to unexpected twists and turns in their lives.

8. Idealistic: Aquarians are idealists at heart, always envisioning a better future and striving to make it a reality. They are driven by their dreams and aspirations, constantly seeking to improve themselves and the world around them.

In conclusion, Aquarians are complex and multi-faceted individuals with a deep sense of humanity and a strong desire to make a positive impact on the world. Their independent spirit, intellectual curiosity, and humanitarian values make them unique and inspiring individuals who are always ready to challenge the status quo and embrace change.

Aquarius in Love and Relationships

Aquarius, the visionary of the zodiac, brings a unique perspective to love and relationships. People born under the Aquarius sign are known for their unconventional approach to romance, their independent nature, and their deep sense of idealism. Understanding how Aquarius approaches love can shed light on their relationships and interactions with others.

Aquarius individuals value intellectual stimulation and meaningful conversations in their relationships. They are attracted to partners who share their progressive views and can engage them in thought-provoking discussions. Aquarians are known for their open-mindedness and acceptance of diversity, making them great partners for those who appreciate freedom and individuality.

In love, Aquarians can be both idealistic and detached. They may have high expectations for their relationships and seek a deep emotional connection with their partners. However, their independent nature and need for personal space can sometimes create challenges in forming close emotional bonds. Aquarians value their freedom and may struggle with traditional ideas of love and commitment.

Communication is key in relationships with Aquarius individuals. They appreciate honesty, transparency, and intellectual compatibility in their partners. Aquarians are known for their humanitarian nature and desire to make the world a better place, so they may be drawn to partners who share their values and social consciousness.

Aquarians are not always the most emotionally expressive individuals, as they tend to prioritize logic and reason over sentimentality. They may show their love through acts of kindness, thoughtful gestures, and supporting their partner's personal growth and aspirations. It's important for Aquarians to find a balance between their intellectual approach to love and their emotional needs to cultivate a fulfilling relationship.

When it comes to compatibility, Aquarius is most compatible with other air signs like Gemini and Libra, who share their intellectual curiosity and love for communication. Fire signs like Aries and Sagittarius can also be a good match for Aquarius, as they bring passion and energy to the relationship. However, Aquarius may struggle in relationships with more emotional and sensitive signs like Cancer and Pisces, as their practical and rational nature may clash with these signs' emotional intensity.

Famous Aquarius personalities like Oprah Winfrey and Ellen DeGeneres exemplify the qualities of Aquarius in love and relationships. They are known for their humanitarian efforts, their progressive views on love and equality, and their ability to connect with others on a deep intellectual level.

In conclusion, Aquarius individuals approach love and relationships with a blend of idealism, independence, and intellectual curiosity. Understanding their unique perspective on romance can help navigate the complexities of love with an Aquarian partner and appreciate the depth and richness they bring to relationships.

Career and Ambitions of Aquarius

Aquarius is known as the visionary of the zodiac, often possessing a unique perspective and unconventional approach to life. Those born under this sign are innovative, forward-thinking, and driven by a strong desire to make a positive impact on the world around them. When it comes to career and ambitions, Aquarians are motivated by their ideals and a deep sense of humanitarianism.

Career Choices:
Aquarians are natural innovators and are drawn to careers that allow them to express their creativity and originality. They thrive in environments that encourage out-of-the-box thinking and value their unique perspectives. Some ideal career paths for Aquarians include technology, science, engineering, social activism, and creative fields such as design and writing.

Ambitions:
Aquarians are ambitious individuals who are driven by their desire to create positive change in society. They often aspire to lead and inspire others, using their visionary ideas to push boundaries and challenge the status quo. Their ambitions are fueled by their strong sense of idealism and their belief in the power of collective action to bring about meaningful transformation.

Professional Traits:
Aquarians are known for their independence, intellectual curiosity, and strong sense of integrity. They are natural leaders who excel in roles that require innovative thinking, problem-solving skills, and a willingness to challenge convention. Aquarians are also highly adaptable and thrive in dynamic and fast-paced work environments.

Work Ethic:
Aquarians are dedicated and hardworking individuals who are committed to their goals and aspirations. They approach their work with a sense of purpose and determination, always striving to make a meaningful impact in their chosen field. They are not afraid to take risks and are willing to push boundaries in pursuit of their ambitions.

Challenges:
Despite their many strengths, Aquarians may face challenges in their careers due to their rebellious nature and tendency to be uncompromising in their beliefs. They may struggle with authority figures or traditional hierarchies, preferring to work independently or in environments that allow them the freedom to express their individuality.

Career Success Strategies:
To achieve success in their careers, Aquarians should focus on leveraging their unique talents and strengths, such as their creativity, innovation, and humanitarian instincts. Developing strong communication skills and fostering collaboration with others can also help Aquarians achieve their ambitious goals. Embracing their idealism while also remaining practical and grounded can lead to long-term career success.

Overall, Aquarians are driven by a deep sense of purpose and a desire to make a positive impact on the world. With their visionary ideas, innovative thinking, and commitment to social progress, Aquarians have the potential to achieve great success in their careers and leave a lasting legacy in their chosen fields.

Strengths and Weaknesses of Aquarius

Aquarius is the eleventh sign of the zodiac, characterized by its innovative and independent nature. People born under the sign of Aquarius, typically between January 20 and February 18, are known for their progressive thinking and humanitarian values. In this section, we will explore the strengths and weaknesses of Aquarius individuals in various aspects of their lives.

Strengths of Aquarius:

1. Intellectual: Aquarians are known for their sharp intellect and analytical abilities. They have a curious mind and are constantly seeking knowledge and understanding of the world around them.

2. Innovative: Aquarians are natural innovators and visionaries. They are often ahead of their time, coming up with new ideas and solutions to complex problems.

3. Independent: Aquarians value their freedom and independence. They are not afraid to think and act outside the box, often marching to the beat of their own drum.

4. Humanitarian: Aquarians are deeply compassionate and care about social causes. They have a strong sense of social justice and are always willing to fight for the greater good.

5. Friendly: Aquarians are known for their friendly and outgoing nature. They have a wide circle of friends and enjoy engaging in meaningful conversations with like-minded individuals.

Weaknesses of Aquarius:

1. Detached: Aquarians can sometimes come across as aloof or detached. They value their independence so much that they may struggle to connect emotionally with others on a deeper level.

2. Stubborn: Aquarians can be quite stubborn and inflexible in their opinions. Once they have made up their mind about something, it can be challenging to convince them otherwise.

3. Rebellious: Aquarians have a rebellious streak and may resist authority or convention. While this can be a strength in terms of innovation, it can also lead to conflicts in certain situations.

4. Unpredictable: Aquarians are known for their unpredictable nature. They may change their plans or opinions at the drop of a hat, which can be disconcerting for those around them.

5. Emotionally Distant: Aquarians may struggle with expressing their emotions openly. They tend to prioritize logic and reason over feelings, which can sometimes lead to misunderstandings in personal relationships.

In conclusion, Aquarians possess a unique blend of strengths and weaknesses that shape their personality and interactions with the world. By embracing their innovative spirit and humanitarian values while being mindful of their potential pitfalls such as detachment and stubbornness, Aquarians can navigate life with a balance of intellect and emotion, making a positive impact on those around them.

Aquarius Compatibility with Other Signs

Aquarius, the visionary of the zodiac, is known for their forward-thinking nature, intellectual prowess, and unique perspective on life. When it comes to compatibility with other signs, Aquarius can form intriguing and dynamic relationships with various zodiac signs due to their open-mindedness and independent spirit.

In romantic relationships, Aquarius is most compatible with fellow air signs - Gemini and Libra. These signs share Aquarius' love for intellectual stimulation, freedom, and social interactions. Gemini's wit and adaptability complement Aquarius' innovative ideas, while Libra's charm and diplomacy create a harmonious partnership with the humanitarian Aquarius.

Aquarius also finds compatibility with fire signs like Aries and Sagittarius. Aries' passion and adventurous spirit resonate well with Aquarius' unconventional approach to life, creating a dynamic and exciting relationship. Sagittarius' optimism and philosophical nature align with Aquarius' quest for knowledge and understanding, making them great partners in exploring new ideas and experiences.

On the other hand, Aquarius may face challenges in relationships with water signs such as Cancer and Pisces. Cancer's emotional depth and sensitivity may clash with Aquarius' rational and detached demeanor, leading to misunderstandings and conflicts. Pisces' dreamy and intuitive nature can sometimes overwhelm the logical Aquarius, making it challenging to find common ground.

In friendships, Aquarius thrives with like-minded individuals who share their passion for social causes and intellectual discussions. Aquarius gets along well with fellow air signs like Gemini and Libra, as they enjoy engaging in thought-provoking conversations and exploring new ideas together. Aquarius also appreciates the loyalty and support of earth signs like Taurus and Capricorn, who provide stability and practical advice to the visionary Aquarius.

In the professional realm, Aquarius excels in collaborative environments where they can express their innovative ideas and work towards a common goal. Aquarius finds success working with creative signs like Leo and Sagittarius, who appreciate their unique perspective and are willing to support their unconventional approach to problem-solving. Aquarius may face challenges in partnerships with more traditional signs like Taurus and Virgo, as their practicality and attention to detail may clash with Aquarius' desire for experimentation and change.

Overall, Aquarius' compatibility with other signs is influenced by their open-mindedness, independence, and innovative spirit. By understanding and embracing the diverse traits of different zodiac signs, Aquarius can form meaningful and fulfilling relationships that foster personal growth and mutual understanding.

Famous Aquarius Personalities

Aquarius is the eleventh sign of the zodiac and is known for its innovative and forward-thinking nature. People born under the sign of Aquarius are often described as independent, eccentric, and humanitarian. They are visionaries who are always looking for ways to make the world a better place. Famous Aquarius personalities embody these traits and have made significant contributions to various fields. Here are some notable Aquarians:

1. Oprah Winfrey - Born on January 29, Oprah Winfrey is a media mogul, philanthropist, and talk show host known for her inspirational messages and impact on society. She is a true Aquarian in her humanitarian efforts, using her platform to raise awareness about important social issues and empower others.

2. Abraham Lincoln - Born on February 12, Abraham Lincoln was the 16th President of the United States and led the country through the Civil War. His progressive and humanitarian views align with the Aquarius traits of equality and social justice.

3. Jennifer Aniston - Born on February 11, Jennifer Aniston is an actress known for her role as Rachel Green on the popular TV show "Friends." She embodies the Aquarius spirit of individuality and originality in her acting career.

4. Bob Marley - Born on February 6, Bob Marley was a legendary reggae musician and songwriter known for his messages of peace, love, and unity. His music continues to inspire people around the world, reflecting the humanitarian values of Aquarius.

5. Ellen DeGeneres - Born on January 26, Ellen DeGeneres is a comedian, actress, and talk show host who is known for her kindness and generosity. She uses her platform to promote positivity and inclusivity, embodying the Aquarian ideals of equality and acceptance.

6. Thomas Edison - Born on February 11, Thomas Edison was an inventor and businessman who is credited with many groundbreaking inventions, including the light bulb and the phonograph. His innovative spirit and forward-thinking approach align with the Aquarius traits of creativity and originality.

7. Shakira - Born on February 2, Shakira is a Colombian singer-songwriter known for her unique voice and fusion of musical styles. She is a passionate advocate for education and child welfare, reflecting the humanitarian values of Aquarius.

8. Cristiano Ronaldo - Born on February 5, Cristiano Ronaldo is a professional footballer considered one of the greatest players of all time. His determination, leadership, and philanthropic efforts showcase the ambitious and humanitarian nature of Aquarius.

These famous Aquarius personalities demonstrate the diverse talents and qualities associated with this zodiac sign. Their contributions to the world reflect the progressive, innovative, and humanitarian spirit of Aquarius, inspiring others to embrace their individuality and work towards positive change.

Chapter 13

Pisces

Pisces Overview and Symbolism

Pisces, the twelfth sign of the zodiac, is represented by the symbol of two fish swimming in opposite directions. This symbol reflects the duality and fluidity of Pisces individuals, who are known for their deep emotions, compassion, and intuitive nature. Those born under the sign of Pisces are often considered the dreamers of the zodiac, as they possess a vivid imagination and a strong connection to the spiritual realm.

Pisces is ruled by the planet Neptune, which governs dreams, illusions, and creativity. This influence gives Pisces a heightened sense of empathy and sensitivity to the world around them. Neptune also brings a mystical quality to Piscean energy, making them deeply intuitive and in tune with their subconscious mind.

One of the key traits of Pisces is their compassionate and selfless nature. They are highly empathetic individuals who are always willing to lend a helping hand to those in need. Pisceans are natural healers and caregivers, drawn to professions that allow them to make a positive impact on others, such as nursing, counseling, or social work.

Pisces individuals are known for their artistic talents and creative abilities. They have a strong imagination and a unique perspective on the world, which often manifests in their artistic pursuits. Whether it be music, painting, writing, or dance, Pisceans have a natural flair for expressing themselves creatively and connecting with others on a deep emotional level.

On the flip side, Pisces can sometimes struggle with boundaries and reality, as they tend to get lost in their own dreams and fantasies. This can lead to escapism and a tendency to avoid facing difficult emotions or situations. Pisceans may also be prone to mood swings and emotional instability, as they absorb the energies of those around them and can easily become overwhelmed by external stimuli.

In relationships, Pisces are romantic and idealistic partners who seek deep emotional connections and spiritual bonds. They are loyal and devoted lovers who are willing to go to great lengths to make their partners happy. However, Pisceans can also be prone to idealizing their partners and may struggle with setting healthy boundaries in relationships.

In conclusion, Pisces is a sign that embodies empathy, creativity, and spiritual depth. Those born under this sign possess a unique blend of sensitivity, compassion, and artistic talent that sets them apart from the rest of the zodiac. While they may face challenges related to boundaries and reality, Pisceans have the ability to tap into their intuition and inner wisdom to navigate life's complexities with grace and compassion.

Personality Traits of Pisces

Pisces, the twelfth and final sign of the zodiac, is represented by the Fish symbol. Individuals born between February 19 and March 20 fall under this water sign ruled by Neptune, the planet of dreams and intuition. Pisceans are known for their compassionate, imaginative, and sensitive nature, making them one of the most empathetic and intuitive signs in the zodiac.

Personality Traits of Pisces:

1. Compassionate and Empathetic: Pisceans have a deep sense of compassion for others and can easily put themselves in someone else's shoes. They are highly empathetic and always willing to lend a helping hand to those in need.

2. Imaginative and Creative: The artistic and creative abilities of Pisceans are boundless. They have a vivid imagination and a strong connection to their inner world, making them excellent artists, writers, musicians, and dreamers.

3. Sensitive and Intuitive: Pisceans are highly sensitive to the emotions of others and their surroundings. They have a keen intuition that guides them in making decisions and understanding the deeper meaning behind situations.

4. Adaptable and Flexible: Being a mutable sign, Pisces is adaptable and flexible, able to go with the flow and adjust to different circumstances effortlessly. They are open-minded and can easily navigate through changes and transitions.

5. Dreamy and Idealistic: Pisceans live in a world of dreams and fantasies, often escaping reality through their rich imagination. They are idealists who believe in the power of love, compassion, and spiritual connections.

6. Selfless and Altruistic: Pisceans have a selfless nature and are always willing to sacrifice their own needs for the well-being of others. They have a strong desire to help and support those around them, making them natural caregivers and nurturers.

7. Emotional and Empathic: Emotions run deep in Pisceans, and they are in tune with their feelings and the emotions of those around them. They can easily pick up on subtle cues and nuances in interpersonal dynamics.

8. Escapist Tendencies: Due to their sensitive and emotional nature, Pisceans may have a tendency to escape reality through various means such as daydreaming, creativity, or even indulging in unhealthy behaviors like substance abuse.

In conclusion, Pisceans are known for their compassionate, imaginative, and sensitive nature. They possess a deep sense of empathy, creativity, and intuition, making them natural healers and dreamers. While their idealistic and dreamy nature can lead them to escapism at times, Pisceans bring a sense of magic and inspiration to the world through their artistic talents and emotional depth.

Pisces in Love and Relationships

Pisces, the twelfth sign of the zodiac, is known for its dreamy and romantic nature. Individuals born under the sign of Pisces are compassionate, sensitive, and deeply empathetic, making them natural nurturers and caregivers in relationships. Here, we delve into the unique characteristics of Pisces when it comes to love and relationships.

Personality Traits of Pisces in Love:
Pisces individuals are incredibly romantic and idealistic when it comes to love. They are intuitive and empathetic, often able to understand their partner's needs and emotions on a profound level. Pisces are selfless lovers who

prioritize the happiness of their partners above their own. Their emotional depth and ability to connect on a spiritual level make them incredibly loving and supportive partners.

Pisces in Love and Relationships:
In relationships, Pisces are loyal and devoted partners who seek deep emotional connections. They are known for their compassionate and nurturing nature, always willing to support their loved ones through thick and thin. Pisces are highly intuitive and empathetic, making them attentive listeners and understanding partners. They thrive in relationships that are based on trust, emotional intimacy, and mutual respect.

Career and Ambitions of Pisces:
In their professional lives, Pisces are often drawn to creative and artistic pursuits. They have a natural talent for expressing themselves through music, art, or writing. Pisces individuals are compassionate and empathetic, making them well-suited for careers in helping professions such as counseling, social work, or healthcare. They are also intuitive and imaginative, which can lead them to success in fields such as film, photography, or design.

Strengths and Weaknesses of Pisces:
Pisces' greatest strengths in relationships lie in their compassion, empathy, and sensitivity. They are deeply romantic and caring partners who prioritize emotional intimacy and connection. However, Pisces' emotional sensitivity can also be a weakness, as they may struggle with boundaries and become easily overwhelmed by the emotions of others. Pisces individuals may also be prone to escapism and idealism, which can sometimes lead to difficulties in facing reality.

Pisces Compatibility with Other Signs:
Pisces are most compatible with other water signs such as Cancer and Scorpio, as well as earth signs like Taurus and Capricorn. These signs share Pisces' emotional depth and need for stability in relationships. Pisces may also find compatibility with fellow mutable signs such as Virgo and Sagittarius, who can appreciate their creativity and sensitivity.

Famous Pisces Personalities:

Some famous Pisces individuals known for their romantic and creative nature include Rihanna, Justin Bieber, and Carrie Underwood. These celebrities embody the compassionate and artistic qualities often associated with Pisces.

In conclusion, Pisces individuals bring a unique blend of compassion, sensitivity, and creativity to their relationships. Their romantic and idealistic nature makes them loving and supportive partners who prioritize emotional intimacy and connection. By understanding Pisces' strengths and weaknesses in love, one can navigate relationships with these intuitive and empathetic individuals with greater understanding and appreciation.

Career and Ambitions of Pisces

As we delve into the chapter on Pisces – The Dreamer, it is important to explore the career and ambitions that are typically associated with individuals born under this compassionate and imaginative zodiac sign.

Pisces individuals are known for their artistic and creative talents, making them well-suited for careers in the arts, music, writing, and design. Their deep emotional sensitivity and empathy allow them to connect with others on a profound level, making them excellent counselors, therapists, and healers. Pisces are also highly intuitive and spiritual, which can lead them to pursue careers in fields such as astrology, metaphysics, and spirituality.

Due to their compassionate nature, Pisces may also excel in humanitarian and charitable work, where they can make a positive impact on the world by helping those in need. They are often drawn to professions that involve caring for others, such as nursing, social work, or non-profit organizations.

In the workplace, Pisces individuals are known for their adaptability and creativity. They are able to navigate complex situations with ease and are often the ones who bring a sense of harmony and peace to their work environment. Pisces are also highly intuitive and can excel in roles that require them to trust their instincts and make decisions based on their gut feelings.

Despite their artistic and sensitive nature, Pisces individuals can also be highly ambitious when it comes to their career goals. They are driven by a desire to make a meaningful impact on the world and may set their sights on achieving success in their chosen field. Pisces individuals are often attracted to roles that allow them to express their creativity and imagination, as well as those that provide them with opportunities for personal growth and development.

In terms of ambitions, Pisces individuals may aspire to create a life that is aligned with their values and beliefs. They seek fulfillment and meaning in their work and are willing to put in the effort to achieve their goals. Pisces individuals may also be drawn to careers that allow them to explore their spiritual side and connect with a higher purpose.

Overall, the career and ambitions of Pisces individuals are characterized by their creativity, empathy, and desire to make a positive impact on the world. They excel in roles that allow them to express their artistic talents, help others, and pursue their passions. By following their intuition and staying true to their values, Pisces individuals can achieve success and fulfillment in their chosen career path.

Strengths and Weaknesses of Pisces

Pisces, the last sign of the zodiac, is represented by two fish swimming in opposite directions, symbolizing the duality and complexity of the Pisces personality. Those born under the sign of Pisces, typically falling between February 19 and March 20, are known for their compassionate and imaginative nature. Let's delve into the strengths and weaknesses of Pisces individuals.

Strengths of Pisces:

1. Compassionate and Empathetic: Pisces are highly empathetic individuals who feel deeply for others. They have a natural inclination towards helping those in need and are known for their compassion and kindness.

2. Intuitive and Creative: Pisces are intuitive beings with a strong creative streak. They often have a vivid imagination and are drawn to artistic pursuits such as music, writing, and visual arts.

3. Sensitive and Emotional: Pisces are in touch with their emotions and are sensitive to the feelings of others. They possess a deep emotional depth that allows them to connect with people on a profound level.

4. Selfless and Altruistic: Pisces are selfless individuals who put the needs of others above their own. They are generous and caring, always willing to lend a helping hand to those in need.

5. Flexible and Adaptive: Pisces are adaptable individuals who can easily go with the flow and adjust to changing circumstances. They are open-minded and willing to try new things, making them versatile in various situations.

Weaknesses of Pisces:

1. Overly Idealistic: Pisces individuals can sometimes be overly idealistic, seeing the world through rose-colored glasses. This can lead to disappointment when reality does not match their romanticized expectations.

2. Escapist Tendencies: Due to their sensitive and emotional nature, Pisces may have a tendency to escape from reality through various means such as daydreaming, substance abuse, or engaging in avoidant behaviors.

3. Indecisive and Overly Trusting: Pisces individuals can struggle with making decisions due to their indecisive nature. They may also be overly trusting of others, making them susceptible to being taken advantage of.

4. Boundary Issues: Pisces individuals have a tendency to merge boundaries with others, sometimes to the detriment of their own well-being. They may struggle to assert themselves and set healthy boundaries in relationships.

5. Prone to Escaping Responsibilities: Pisces individuals may have a tendency to avoid facing responsibilities or dealing with practical matters. Their escapist tendencies can sometimes lead to procrastination and difficulty in handling day-to-day tasks.

In conclusion, Pisces individuals possess a unique blend of strengths and weaknesses that shape their personality and interactions with the world. By understanding and embracing these qualities, Pisces individuals can navigate life's challenges and harness their strengths to fulfill their potential.

Pisces Compatibility with Other Signs

Pisces, the last sign of the zodiac, is known for its dreamy and compassionate nature. People born under the sign of Pisces are imaginative, empathetic, and sensitive individuals who are deeply in tune with their emotions and the emotions of others. When it comes to compatibility with other signs, Pisces can form strong and meaningful relationships with a variety of personalities due to their adaptable and understanding nature.

Pisces and Aries: Pisces and Aries are considered to be an interesting match as they possess complementary traits. Aries can benefit from Pisces' emotional depth and intuition, while Pisces can find stability and strength in Aries' assertiveness. However, conflicts may arise due to Aries' impulsive nature conflicting with Pisces' desire for harmony.

Pisces and Taurus: Pisces and Taurus share a deep emotional connection and a love for beauty and comfort. Taurus' grounded nature can provide stability for the sometimes flighty Pisces, while Pisces can help Taurus tap into their more imaginative and creative side. This pairing can create a harmonious and nurturing relationship.

Pisces and Gemini: Pisces and Gemini have different approaches to life, with Pisces being more intuitive and emotional, while Gemini is more intellectual and communicative. While they may have fun and stimulating conversations, conflicts can arise due to Pisces' sensitivity and Gemini's tendency to be detached.

Pisces and Cancer: Pisces and Cancer are both water signs, which means they share a deep emotional understanding and connection. They can create a loving and nurturing relationship based on mutual compassion and empathy. Both signs value emotional security and can provide each other with the support and care they need.

Pisces and Leo: Pisces and Leo have contrasting personalities, with Pisces being sensitive and introverted, while Leo is confident and outgoing. While they may be attracted to each other's differences initially, maintaining a long-term relationship may require compromise and understanding to bridge the gap between their personalities.

Pisces and Virgo: Pisces and Virgo are opposite signs in the zodiac, which can create a complementary dynamic. Virgo's practicality can balance Pisces' dreaminess, while Pisces can help Virgo tap into their emotional side. Communication and mutual understanding are key to making this relationship work.

Pisces and Libra: Pisces and Libra share a love for beauty, harmony, and romance, which can create a strong bond between them. Both signs are compassionate and empathetic, making them good listeners and supportive partners for each other. However, conflicts may arise due to Pisces' emotional intensity and Libra's need for balance and fairness.

Pisces and Scorpio: Pisces and Scorpio are both water signs, which means they share a deep emotional connection and understanding. They can form a passionate and intense relationship based on mutual trust and emotional depth. Both signs are intuitive and empathetic, making them highly attuned to each other's needs.

Pisces and Sagittarius: Pisces and Sagittarius have different approaches to life, with Pisces being emotional and intuitive, while Sagittarius is adventurous and independent. While they may be drawn to each other's differences, conflicts can arise due to Pisces' sensitivity and Sagittarius' blunt honesty.

Pisces and Capricorn: Pisces and Capricorn have contrasting personalities, with Pisces being intuitive and dreamy, while Capricorn is practical and ambitious. They can complement each other well, with Pisces providing emotional support and creativity, while Capricorn offers stability and structure. Communication and compromise are essential for this relationship to thrive.

Overall, Pisces can form meaningful connections with a variety of signs due to their compassionate and understanding nature. By embracing their emotional depth and intuition, Pisces can navigate the complexities of relationships with grace and empathy, making them valued partners and friends in the zodiac.

Famous Pisces Personalities

Pisces, the 12th and final sign of the zodiac, is known for its dreamy and compassionate nature. Those born under the sign of Pisces are often artistic, intuitive, and empathetic individuals. Let's explore some famous Pisces personalities who have left a mark on the world with their talents and accomplishments.

One notable Pisces personality is the renowned artist and inventor, Leonardo da Vinci. Born on March 15, 1452, da Vinci was a true Renaissance man, excelling in fields such as painting, sculpture, anatomy, engineering, and architecture. His most famous works include the Mona Lisa and The Last Supper, which continue to inspire art lovers around the globe.

Another iconic Pisces is music legend, Rihanna. Born on February 20, 1988, the Barbadian singer-songwriter has achieved immense success in the music industry with hits like "Umbrella," "Diamonds," and "Work." Known for her versatile voice and bold fashion choices, Rihanna has also ventured into acting, fashion design, and philanthropy, solidifying her status as a global icon.

Actor and humanitarian, Steve Jobs, is also a notable Pisces personality. Born on February 24, 1955, Jobs co-founded Apple Inc. and played a pivotal role in revolutionizing the technology industry with products like the iPhone, iPad, and Macintosh computer. His innovative vision and relentless pursuit of excellence have left an indelible mark on the world of technology.

The talented actress and producer, Drew Barrymore, is another Pisces who has captivated audiences with her performances on screen. Born on February 22, 1975, Barrymore rose to fame as a child star in films like E.T. the Extra-Terrestrial and went on to establish herself as a successful actress and producer in Hollywood. Known for her charm and versatility, Barrymore continues to inspire fans with her work in film and television.

In the world of literature, Pisces author Dr. Seuss (Theodor Seuss Geisel) stands out for his imaginative and whimsical stories that have enchanted readers of all ages. Born on March 2, 1904, Dr. Seuss is best known for classics such as "The Cat in the Hat," "Green Eggs and Ham," and "How the Grinch Stole Christmas!" His unique storytelling style and colorful illustrations have made him a beloved figure in children's literature.

These famous Pisces personalities demonstrate the diverse talents and strengths associated with this water sign. From creativity and innovation to compassion and empathy, Pisces individuals have made significant contributions to various fields, leaving a lasting legacy that continues to inspire and uplift others.

Chapter 14

The Influence of the Moon and Rising Signs

Understanding the Moon Sign

The Moon plays a significant role in astrology, representing our emotions, inner self, instincts, and subconscious mind. In astrology, the Moon sign is just as important as the Sun sign, as it reveals a deeper layer of a person's personality and emotional needs. Understanding your Moon sign can provide valuable insights into how you process emotions, make decisions, and navigate the world around you.

The Moon sign in your birth chart reflects your emotional nature and how you respond to situations on a deep, instinctual level. It influences your immediate reactions, habits, and emotional patterns. While the Sun sign represents your outward personality and ego, the Moon sign represents your inner self and emotional landscape.

Each zodiac sign is associated with a unique set of emotional characteristics based on the element and qualities of that sign. For example, a person with a Moon in fire signs like Aries, Leo, or Sagittarius may have a passionate and spontaneous emotional nature, while someone with a Moon in earth signs like Taurus, Virgo, or Capricorn may be more grounded and practical in their emotional expressions.

Understanding your Moon sign can help you navigate your emotional world more effectively. By knowing your emotional triggers and needs, you can cultivate self-awareness and make conscious choices that align with your emotional well-being. For example, if you have a Moon in water signs like Cancer, Scorpio, or Pisces, you may be highly sensitive and empathetic, requiring time alone to recharge and process your feelings.

The Moon sign also influences your relationships and how you connect with others on an emotional level. Compatibility between Moon signs can play a crucial role in the dynamics of relationships, as it determines how well two individuals understand and support each other's emotional needs. For instance, a person with a Moon in air signs like Gemini, Libra, or Aquarius may seek intellectual stimulation and communication in their relationships.

In addition to understanding your own Moon sign, it is essential to consider the Moon signs of those around you, such as family members, friends, and romantic partners. By recognizing and respecting each other's emotional needs, you can cultivate healthier and more fulfilling relationships based on empathy and mutual understanding.

Moreover, the Moon sign influences your daily routines, habits, and reactions to changes in your environment. By aligning your activities with the energy of your Moon sign, you can enhance your emotional well-being and overall sense of fulfillment. For example, someone with a Moon in earth signs may find comfort in establishing routines and creating a sense of stability in their daily lives.

In conclusion, understanding your Moon sign is a valuable tool for self-discovery and personal growth. By exploring the emotional landscape of your Moon sign, you can gain deeper insights into your inner world, relationships, and daily experiences. Embracing and honoring your Moon sign can lead to greater emotional awareness, resilience, and authenticity in all areas of your life.

How the Moon Sign Affects Personality and Emotions

The Moon sign in astrology plays a crucial role in shaping an individual's emotional landscape and personality traits. While the Sun sign represents the core essence of a person's identity, the Moon sign delves deeper into one's emotional responses, inner world, and instinctual reactions. Understanding how the Moon sign influences personality and emotions can provide valuable insights into an individual's emotional needs, reactions, and overall emotional well-being.

The Moon sign represents our emotional core, revealing how we process and express our feelings, as well as how we nurture ourselves and others. It reflects our subconscious mind, instincts, and emotional patterns that are deeply ingrained within us. Just as the Moon in the sky governs the tides and influences the ebb and flow of emotions, the Moon sign in our birth chart governs our emotional tides and influences our emotional responses.

Each zodiac sign has a unique way of expressing emotions and processing feelings, and this is where the Moon sign comes into play. For example, a person with a Moon in fiery Aries may have a quick temper and a need for independence in emotional matters, while someone with a Moon in nurturing Cancer may be highly sensitive, caring, and deeply connected to their family and home life.

The Moon sign also reveals our emotional needs and how we seek to fulfill them. For instance, a person with a Moon in practical Taurus may find emotional security through material comforts and stability, while someone with a Moon in intellectual Aquarius may seek emotional fulfillment through social causes and innovative ideas.

Moreover, the Moon sign influences how we react to situations and how we cope with challenges. It can shed light on our gut reactions, instincts, and coping mechanisms when faced with stress or conflict. For instance, a person with a Moon in analytical Virgo may respond to emotional turmoil by seeking practical solutions and analyzing their feelings, while a person with a Moon in intense Scorpio may be more inclined to delve deep into their emotions and seek transformation through emotional catharsis.

Understanding your Moon sign can also help you navigate your relationships and interactions with others. It can provide insights into your emotional compatibility with different people and how you can best support and nurture yourself and others emotionally.

In conclusion, the Moon sign is a significant component of astrology that influences our emotional landscape, instinctual responses, and inner world. By exploring and understanding your Moon sign, you can gain a deeper insight into your emotional needs, reactions, and overall emotional well-being, ultimately leading to greater self-awareness and personal growth.

The Importance of the Rising Sign (Ascendant)

The Rising Sign, also known as the Ascendant, is a crucial component in astrology as it represents the way we present ourselves to the world, our first impressions, and our overall approach to life. While the Sun sign reveals our core essence and the Moon sign reflects our emotions and inner self, the Rising Sign is like the mask we wear when interacting with others and the world at large.

One key aspect of the Rising Sign is that it determines the cusp of the first house in the natal chart, which sets the stage for the rest of the houses and planets in the chart. It forms the foundation upon which the rest of the chart is built, influencing our personality traits, physical appearance, and how we respond to different situations.

The Rising Sign is calculated based on the exact time and place of birth, just like the Sun and Moon signs. It changes approximately every two hours, making it highly specific to an individual. This is why knowing your exact time of birth is crucial in determining your Rising Sign accurately.

In terms of personality traits, the Rising Sign often colors the way we project ourselves to the world. For example, a person with an Aries Rising may come across as assertive and dynamic, while someone with a Pisces Rising may appear more dreamy and sensitive. This initial impression can greatly influence how others perceive us and how we navigate social interactions.

The Rising Sign also plays a role in shaping our physical appearance. While the Sun sign may influence our overall essence and personality, the Rising Sign can impact our external appearance and demeanor. For instance, a Taurus Rising individual may have a strong, sturdy build and a calm, steady presence, reflecting the earthy and grounded qualities associated with Taurus.

Furthermore, the Rising Sign can provide valuable insights into our approach to life and our general outlook. It can indicate our natural instincts, our immediate reactions to situations, and our overall attitude towards challenges and opportunities. Understanding your Rising Sign can help you align with your authentic self and make conscious choices that resonate with your true nature.

Astrologers often consider the Rising Sign when analyzing a birth chart, as it sets the tone for the entire chart interpretation. By understanding the characteristics and significance of the Rising Sign, individuals can gain a deeper understanding of themselves and how they interact with the world around them.

In conclusion, the Rising Sign, or Ascendant, is a fundamental element in astrology that sheds light on how we present ourselves to the world, our initial reactions to life experiences, and our overall demeanor. By delving into the qualities and influences of the Rising Sign, individuals can enhance their self-awareness, improve their relationships, and navigate life with a deeper sense of authenticity and purpose.

How the Rising Sign Influences Appearance and First Impressions

The rising sign, also known as the ascendant sign, plays a crucial role in shaping an individual's appearance and first impressions. While the Sun sign represents the core essence of a person's personality, the rising sign governs how others perceive and interact with them on a surface level. Understanding how the rising sign influences appearance and first impressions can provide valuable insights into how one presents themselves to the world.

The rising sign is the zodiac sign that was rising on the eastern horizon at the moment of a person's birth. It changes approximately every two hours, making it highly specific to an individual's birth time and location. This sign sets the stage for the rest of the birth chart and represents the mask or facade that a person wears in social situations. As a result, it significantly impacts how others perceive an individual upon first meeting them.

In terms of appearance, the rising sign can manifest in physical characteristics and demeanor. For example, an Aries rising individual may have a bold and energetic presence, with sharp features and a strong jawline. Their body language might be assertive and direct, reflecting the assertive and competitive nature of Aries. On the other hand, a Pisces rising person may have a dreamy and ethereal quality to their appearance, with soft and compassionate features. Their mannerisms may be gentle and empathetic, reflecting the sensitive and intuitive nature of Pisces.

Furthermore, the rising sign influences one's style and fashion choices. Individuals with a Leo rising, for instance, may gravitate towards bold and glamorous clothing that helps them command attention and express their creativity. In contrast, a Capricorn rising person may prefer classic and sophisticated attire that conveys professionalism and status. The rising sign not only shapes one's physical appearance but also influences the way they present themselves to the world through their clothing and grooming choices.

Beyond physical appearance, the rising sign also influences first impressions. People often form initial judgments based on a person's demeanor, energy, and overall vibe, all of which are influenced by the rising sign. For example, a Gemini rising individual may come across as witty, curious, and sociable, sparking engaging conversations and connections with others. In contrast, a Scorpio rising person may exude intensity, mystery, and depth, drawing others in with their magnetic presence and enigmatic aura.

Understanding how the rising sign influences appearance and first impressions can help individuals leverage their strengths and navigate social interactions more effectively. By embracing and embodying the qualities of their rising sign, individuals can enhance their personal presentation and make a lasting impact on those they encounter. Ultimately, the rising sign serves as a powerful tool for self-awareness and self-expression, allowing individuals to project their best selves to the world and leave a memorable impression on others.

Chapter 15

The Role of Planetary Aspects and Houses

An Introduction to Planetary Aspects

In astrology, planetary aspects play a crucial role in determining the overall energy and dynamics of an individual's birth chart. These aspects refer to the angles formed between planets in the sky at the time of a person's birth, indicating how the different planetary energies interact with each other. Understanding planetary aspects is essential for gaining deeper insights into an individual's personality, relationships, and life experiences.

There are several types of planetary aspects that astrologers analyze when interpreting a birth chart. The most common aspects include conjunctions, oppositions, squares, trines, and sextiles, each representing a unique energy exchange between planets.

Conjunctions occur when two planets are in close proximity to each other, blending their energies and intensifying their influence on the individual's personality traits and life experiences. This aspect indicates a strong connection between the planets involved, highlighting areas of focus and potential challenges in the person's life.

Oppositions occur when two planets are directly across from each other in the zodiac, creating a push-pull dynamic between their energies. Individuals with opposition aspects in their birth chart may experience internal conflicts or external challenges that require balance and integration of contrasting forces.

Squares are formed when two planets are 90 degrees apart, creating tension and obstacles that need to be overcome. This aspect often indicates areas of friction and internal conflict, prompting personal growth and challenges that lead to transformation and development.

Trines occur when two planets are 120 degrees apart, forming a harmonious flow of energy that supports creativity, opportunities, and positive outcomes. Individuals with trine aspects in their birth chart may have natural talents and abilities that are easily expressed and integrated into their lives.

Sextiles are formed when two planets are 60 degrees apart, facilitating communication and cooperation between their energies. This aspect encourages growth, learning, and new opportunities, providing a harmonious flow of energy that supports personal development and expansion.

Analyzing planetary aspects in a birth chart allows astrologers to uncover hidden patterns, strengths, and challenges that shape an individual's life journey. By understanding how the planets interact with each other, astrologers can provide valuable insights into a person's relationships, career path, and overall life purpose.

Overall, planetary aspects are a fundamental component of astrology that helps individuals gain a deeper understanding of themselves and navigate life's challenges and opportunities with greater awareness and insight. By exploring the dynamics of planetary aspects in a birth chart, individuals can unlock their true potential and align with the cosmic energies that influence their destiny.

Major Aspects and Their Meanings

In astrology, planetary aspects are angles that form between planets in a birth chart. These aspects play a crucial role in determining the overall energy and dynamics of a person's personality, relationships, and life experiences. Understanding major aspects and their meanings is essential for gaining insights into how different planets interact with each other and influence various areas of life.

1. Conjunction (0 degrees): A conjunction occurs when two planets are in close proximity to each other in the same sign. This aspect represents a blending of energies, intensifying the qualities of the planets involved. It can signify a strong focus on a particular area of life or personality traits.

2. Opposition (180 degrees): An opposition happens when two planets are directly across from each other in the zodiac. This aspect signifies a tug-of-war between the energies of the planets, highlighting potential conflicts or challenges in balancing opposing forces in one's life.

3. Square (90 degrees): A square occurs when two planets are separated by 90 degrees in the zodiac. This aspect represents tension, obstacles, and challenges that may arise between the planets involved. It indicates the need for growth and resolution of conflicting energies.

4. Trine (120 degrees): A trine forms when two planets are separated by 120 degrees in the zodiac. This harmonious aspect signifies ease, flow, and positive reinforcement between the planets. It indicates natural talents, opportunities, and areas of support in one's life.

5. Sextile (60 degrees): A sextile occurs when two planets are separated by 60 degrees in the zodiac. This aspect represents opportunities, creativity, and potential for growth between the planets. It indicates favorable circumstances and ease in expressing the energies of the planets involved.

6. Quincunx or Inconjunct (150 degrees): A quincunx forms when two planets are separated by 150 degrees in the zodiac. This aspect signifies adjustments, awkwardness, and a need for integration between the energies of the planets. It highlights areas where compromise and adaptability are required.

7. Semi-Sextile (30 degrees): A semi-sextile occurs when two planets are separated by 30 degrees in the zodiac. This minor aspect represents subtle connections and opportunities for cooperation between the planets. It indicates potential for growth and integration in specific areas of life.

Understanding major aspects and their meanings allows astrologers and individuals to interpret the complex interplay of planetary energies in a birth chart. By analyzing how planets interact through aspects, one can gain valuable insights into personality traits, relationships, and life events. Each aspect carries its unique symbolism and influences, contributing to the overall tapestry of an individual's astrological profile. By exploring and interpreting major aspects in a birth chart, one can deepen their understanding of the intricate patterns and dynamics at play in astrology.

The Twelve Houses of the Zodiac

The Twelve Houses of the Zodiac are a fundamental concept in astrology that plays a crucial role in understanding a person's life experiences, personality traits, and potential outcomes. Each house represents a different aspect of life and corresponds to a specific area of an individual's existence. Understanding the significance of the twelve houses can provide valuable insights into how planetary energies manifest in different areas of one's life.

1. The First House: The House of Self

The First House, also known as the Ascendant or Rising Sign, represents the self, personality, appearance, and how one presents themselves to the world. It is the house of self-awareness, personal identity, and the image we project to others. Planets in the First House influence our self-image and how we approach new beginnings.

2. The Second House: The House of Finances and Values

The Second House governs material possessions, financial security, values, self-worth, and resources. It reflects how we earn, spend, and manage money, as well as our attitudes towards material possessions. Planets in the Second House can influence our financial status and relationship with material wealth.

3. The Third House: The House of Communication and Siblings

The Third House rules communication, intellect, learning, siblings, short trips, and local environment. It represents how we express ourselves verbally, our communication style, and relationships with siblings and neighbors. Planets in the Third House influence our communication skills and intellectual pursuits.

4. The Fourth House: The House of Home and Family

The Fourth House is associated with home, family, roots, ancestry, emotional foundations, and inner security. It reflects our upbringing, family dynamics, and sense of belonging. Planets in the Fourth House influence our relationship with family members and our need for emotional security.

5. The Fifth House: The House of Creativity and Romance

The Fifth House governs creativity, self-expression, romance, children, pleasure, and entertainment. It represents our artistic talents, hobbies, love affairs, and desire for fun and enjoyment. Planets in the Fifth House influence our creative pursuits, romantic relationships, and capacity for joy.

6. The Sixth House: The House of Health and Service

The Sixth House is associated with health, work, service, routines, and daily responsibilities. It reflects our work ethic, habits, physical well-being, and attitude towards service to others. Planets in the Sixth House influence our approach to work, health practices, and daily routines.

7. The Seventh House: The House of Partnerships

The Seventh House governs partnerships, marriage, relationships, contracts, and open enemies. It represents our significant others, business partners, and how we relate to others on a one-on-one basis. Planets in the Seventh House influence our relationships and partnerships.

8. The Eighth House: The House of Transformation and Shared Resources

The Eighth House rules transformation, intimacy, shared resources, inheritance, and psychological growth. It reflects our attitudes towards sex, death, rebirth, and shared finances. Planets in the Eighth House influence our ability to transform and regenerate.

9. The Ninth House: The House of Philosophy and Higher Learning

The Ninth House is associated with philosophy, higher education, long-distance travel, spirituality, and beliefs. It represents our quest for knowledge, spiritual growth, and exploration of higher truths. Planets in the Ninth House influence our perspective on life and thirst for wisdom.

10. The Tenth House: The House of Career and Public Image

The Tenth House governs career, public life, reputation, achievements, authority figures, and social status. It reflects our ambitions, professional goals, and how we are perceived in the public eye. Planets in the Tenth House influence our career path and aspirations.

11. The Eleventh House: The House of Friendships and Goals

The Eleventh House rules friendships, groups, social networks, aspirations, ideals, and humanitarian causes. It represents our friendships, social circles, and collective goals. Planets in the Eleventh House influence our social connections and involvement in group activities.

12. The Twelfth House: The House of Subconscious and Endings

The Twelfth House is associated with the subconscious mind, solitude, hidden enemies, karma, and endings. It reflects our hidden fears, past life experiences, and spiritual transcendence. Planets in the Twelfth House influence our subconscious patterns and spiritual evolution.

Understanding the significance of each of the twelve houses in the zodiac can provide valuable insights into different aspects of a person's life and help individuals navigate challenges, capitalize on opportunities, and achieve personal growth and fulfillment. By examining the placement of planets in each house of the natal chart, astrologers can offer guidance on how to harness planetary energies to enhance various areas of life and optimize individual potential.

The Role of Planetary Aspects and Houses

In astrology, the placement of planets in different houses within the zodiac chart plays a significant role in influencing various aspects of an individual's life. Each planet represents different energies and characteristics, and when situated in specific houses, they can have a profound impact on an individual's personality, behavior, and life experiences.

The Twelve Houses of the Zodiac:
The zodiac chart is divided into twelve houses, each representing different areas of life and aspects of one's personality. The planets' placement in these houses can provide insights into how these energies manifest in specific areas of an individual's life. Here is a brief overview of the twelve houses and the areas they represent:

1. The First House (House of Self): This house governs self-image, personality, and how one presents themselves to the world. Planets in the first house can influence one's identity and outward expression.

2. The Second House (House of Finances): This house relates to material possessions, finances, and self-worth. Planets here can impact one's attitude towards money and possessions.

3. The Third House (House of Communication): This house governs communication, learning, and relationships with siblings. Planets in the third house can influence how one communicates and processes information.

4. The Fourth House (House of Home and Family): This house represents roots, family, and emotional foundations. Planets here can influence one's relationship with family and sense of security.

5. The Fifth House (House of Creativity and Romance): This house governs creativity, self-expression, and love affairs. Planets in the fifth house can impact one's creativity and romantic pursuits.

6. The Sixth House (House of Health and Service): This house relates to work, health, and daily routines. Planets here can influence one's approach to work and well-being.

7. The Seventh House (House of Partnerships): This house governs relationships, partnerships, and marriage. Planets in the seventh house can impact one's interactions with others and approach to relationships.

8. The Eighth House (House of Transformation): This house represents transformation, shared resources, and intimacy. Planets here can influence one's attitude towards change and shared assets.

9. The Ninth House (House of Philosophy and Higher Learning): This house relates to beliefs, higher education, and travel. Planets in the ninth house can impact one's worldview and spiritual beliefs.

10. The Tenth House (House of Career and Public Image): This house governs career, reputation, and public life. Planets here can influence one's ambitions and public image.

11. The Eleventh House (House of Friendship and Goals): This house represents friendships, social groups, and aspirations. Planets in the eleventh house can impact one's social life and goals.

12. The Twelfth House (House of Subconscious): This house relates to the subconscious mind, spirituality, and hidden strengths. Planets here can influence one's inner world and spiritual growth.

How Planets in Houses Influence Your Life:
The placement of planets in different houses can provide valuable insights into how these energies manifest in specific areas of your life. For example, if Mars, the planet of action and energy, is located in your fourth house of home and family, you may be driven to take assertive actions to protect and nurture your family members. Similarly, if Venus, the planet of love and relationships, is situated in your seventh house of partnerships, you may place a strong emphasis on harmonious and loving relationships in your life.

Each planet's placement in a specific house can highlight strengths, challenges, and opportunities in various aspects of your life. By understanding how planets influence different areas of your life, you can gain deeper insights into your personality, behavior, and life experiences. Astrology offers a valuable tool for self-reflection and personal growth by providing a framework to better understand the complexities of human nature and the interconnectedness of planetary energies in shaping our lives.

Chapter 16

Zodiac Signs and Health

Aries to Pisces: Health Strengths and Vulnerabilities

Aries (March 21 - April 19):
Health Strengths: Aries individuals are known for their high energy levels and physical vitality. They are generally active and enjoy engaging in physical activities, which helps them maintain good cardiovascular health. Aries are also resilient and have a strong immune system, enabling them to recover quickly from illnesses.

Health Vulnerabilities: Despite their robust constitution, Aries individuals may face health challenges related to their impulsive nature. They are prone to accidents and injuries due to their tendency to act before thinking. Aries may also experience issues with their head, face, and eyes, so it's essential for them to take precautions and avoid reckless behavior.

Taurus (April 20 - May 20):
Health Strengths: Taurus individuals have a strong and steady constitution, which contributes to their overall physical endurance. They are known for their love of indulgent foods, but they also have a good metabolism that helps them maintain a healthy weight. Taurus individuals are also grounded and stable, which can have a positive impact on their mental health.

Health Vulnerabilities: Taurus individuals may experience health issues related to their indulgent tendencies, such as weight gain and digestive problems. They are also prone to stubbornness, which can make it challenging for them to adopt healthier habits. Taurus individuals should pay attention to their diet and exercise regularly to maintain their overall well-being.

Gemini (May 21 - June 20):
Health Strengths: Gemini individuals are typically agile and quick-witted, which can contribute to their overall physical health. They have a curious nature that may lead them to explore different forms of exercise and activities, keeping them mentally and physically stimulated. Gemini individuals are also good communicators, which can positively impact their mental health.

Health Vulnerabilities: Gemini individuals may face health challenges related to their restless nature. They are prone to stress and anxiety due to their active minds, which can affect their overall well-being. Gemini individuals should prioritize relaxation techniques and mindfulness practices to maintain their mental and emotional health.

Cancer (June 21 - July 22):

Health Strengths: Cancer individuals are nurturing and caring, which can have a positive impact on their overall well-being. They are intuitive and sensitive, allowing them to listen to their bodies and address any health concerns promptly. Cancer individuals also have strong emotional support systems, which can help them cope with stress and maintain mental health.

Health Vulnerabilities: Cancer individuals may experience health issues related to their tendency to hold onto emotions. They are prone to digestive problems and mood swings, which can affect their overall health. Cancer individuals should focus on expressing their emotions and seeking support when needed to maintain their physical and emotional well-being.

Leo (July 23 - August 22):

Health Strengths: Leo individuals are confident and charismatic, which can positively impact their overall health. They have a strong sense of self-esteem, which can boost their immune system and promote overall well-being. Leo individuals are also creative and passionate, allowing them to engage in activities that bring them joy and fulfillment.

Health Vulnerabilities: Leo individuals may face health challenges related to their need for attention and validation. They are prone to stress and burnout due to their ambitious nature. Leo individuals should prioritize self-care and relaxation to prevent physical and mental health issues.

Virgo (August 23 - September 22):

Health Strengths: Virgo individuals are meticulous and detail-oriented, which can have a positive impact on their overall health. They pay attention to their diet, exercise, and wellness routines, promoting good physical health. Virgo individuals are also analytical and practical, which can help them address health concerns proactively.

Health Vulnerabilities: Virgo individuals may experience health issues related to their tendency towards perfectionism. They are prone to anxiety and stress due to their high standards. Virgo individuals should focus on self-compassion and flexibility to maintain their mental and emotional well-being.

Libra (September 23 - October 22):
Health Strengths: Libra individuals are diplomatic and harmonious, which can positively impact their overall health. They prioritize balance and moderation in their lifestyle, promoting physical and mental well-being. Libra individuals are also social and enjoy connecting with others, which can have a positive impact on their mental health.

Health Vulnerabilities: Libra individuals may face health challenges related to their indecisiveness and tendency to avoid conflict. They are prone to stress and may experience issues with their kidneys and lower back. Libra individuals should focus on stress management techniques and assertiveness to maintain their overall well-being.

Scorpio (October 23 - November 21):
Health Strengths: Scorpio individuals are intense and focused, which can have a positive impact on their overall health. They are resilient and determined, enabling them to overcome health challenges. Scorpio individuals are also intuitive and perceptive, which allows them to listen to their bodies and address any health concerns promptly.

Health Vulnerabilities: Scorpio individuals may face health issues related to their tendency towards extremes. They are prone to emotional intensity and may experience issues with their reproductive system. Scorpio individuals should focus on moderation and emotional balance to maintain their physical and mental well-being.

Sagittarius (November 22 - December 21):
Health Strengths: Sagittarius individuals are adventurous and optimistic, which can positively impact their overall health. They enjoy exploring new activities and experiences, keeping them mentally and physically stimulated. Sagittarius individuals are also philosophical and open-minded, which can have a positive impact on their mental health.

Health Vulnerabilities: Sagittarius individuals may face health challenges related to their tendency to overindulge. They are prone to excess, which can lead to issues with their liver and hips. Sagittarius individuals should focus on moderation and self-discipline to maintain their overall well-being.

Capricorn (December 22 - January 19):

Health Strengths: Capricorn individuals are disciplined and determined, which can have a positive impact on their overall health. They are practical and responsible, prioritizing their well-being and longevity. Capricorn individuals are also ambitious and goal-oriented, which can motivate them to maintain healthy lifestyle habits.

Health Vulnerabilities: Capricorn individuals may face health issues related to their tendency towards workaholism. They are prone to stress and may experience issues with their bones and joints. Capricorn individuals should prioritize work-life balance and relaxation to prevent physical and mental health issues.

Aquarius (January 20 - February 18):

Health Strengths: Aquarius individuals are innovative and humanitarian, which can positively impact their overall health. They are open-minded and enjoy exploring alternative health practices, keeping them mentally and physically stimulated. Aquarius individuals are also social and enjoy connecting with others, which can have a positive impact on their mental health.

Health Vulnerabilities: Aquarius individuals may face health challenges related to their rebellious nature. They are prone to sudden changes and may experience issues with their circulatory system. Aquarius individuals should focus on consistency and self-care to maintain their overall well-being.

Pisces (February 19 - March 20):

Health Strengths: Pisces individuals are compassionate and intuitive, which can have a positive impact on their overall health. They have a strong connection to their emotions and inner world, enabling them to address any health concerns promptly. Pisces individuals are also creative and imaginative, which can promote mental well-being.

Health Vulnerabilities: Pisces individuals may face health issues related to their sensitive nature. They are prone to escapism and may experience issues with addiction and immune system disorders. Pisces individuals should focus on healthy coping mechanisms and boundaries to maintain their physical and emotional well-being.

Overall, understanding the health strengths and vulnerabilities of each zodiac sign can provide valuable insights into how individuals can maintain their well-being. By recognizing their inherent tendencies and taking proactive steps to address potential health challenges, individuals can optimize their physical and mental health based on their astrological sign.

Tips for Maintaining Wellness Based on Your Zodiac Sign

Maintaining wellness is a holistic practice that involves taking care of your physical, mental, and emotional well-being. In astrology, each zodiac sign has unique characteristics and tendencies that can influence how individuals approach their health and wellness routines. By understanding the specific needs and challenges associated with your zodiac sign, you can tailor your wellness practices to better support your overall health and vitality.

Aries (March 21 - April 19): Aries individuals are known for their high energy levels and competitive nature. To maintain wellness, Aries should focus on activities that channel their excess energy in a positive way, such as intense workouts or competitive sports. However, it's important for Aries to also incorporate relaxation techniques to prevent burnout and manage stress.

Taurus (April 20 - May 20): Taurus individuals are known for their love of comfort and indulgence. To maintain wellness, Taurus should focus on creating a balanced routine that includes healthy meals, regular exercise, and plenty of rest. Taurus should also prioritize self-care practices that promote relaxation and stress relief.

Gemini (May 21 - June 20): Gemini individuals are known for their adaptability and social nature. To maintain wellness, Gemini should focus on incorporating variety into their routine to prevent boredom and stagnation. Engaging in activities that stimulate the mind, such as reading or learning new skills, can also help Gemini maintain mental wellness.

Cancer (June 21 - July 22): Cancer individuals are known for their nurturing and sensitive nature. To maintain wellness, Cancer should focus on creating a supportive environment that promotes emotional well-being. Practicing self-care rituals and setting boundaries with others can help Cancer maintain a sense of balance and emotional stability.

Leo (July 23 - August 22): Leo individuals are known for their confidence and charisma. To maintain wellness, Leo should focus on activities that boost their self-esteem and creativity, such as performing arts or creative hobbies. It's important for Leo to also prioritize relaxation and self-care to prevent burnout.

Virgo (August 23 - September 22): Virgo individuals are known for their attention to detail and perfectionist tendencies. To maintain wellness, Virgo should focus on creating a structured routine that includes healthy habits and self-care practices. It's important for Virgo to also practice self-compassion and flexibility to prevent excessive stress and anxiety.

Libra (September 23 - October 22): Libra individuals are known for their love of beauty and harmony. To maintain wellness, Libra should focus on creating a balanced lifestyle that includes regular exercise, healthy relationships, and self-care practices. It's important for Libra to also prioritize self-expression and creativity to maintain emotional well-being.

Scorpio (October 23 - November 21): Scorpio individuals are known for their intensity and passion. To maintain wellness, Scorpio should focus on activities that promote emotional healing and transformation, such as therapy or introspective practices. It's important for Scorpio to also practice healthy boundaries and self-care to prevent emotional burnout.

Sagittarius (November 22 - December 21): Sagittarius individuals are known for their adventurous spirit and love of freedom. To maintain wellness, Sagittarius should focus on activities that promote personal growth and exploration, such as travel or learning new skills. It's important for Sagittarius to also prioritize self-reflection and mindfulness to maintain emotional balance.

Capricorn (December 22 - January 19): Capricorn individuals are known for their ambition and discipline. To maintain wellness, Capricorn should focus on creating a balanced routine that includes time for relaxation and self-care. It's important for Capricorn to also practice self-compassion and flexibility to prevent burnout and maintain emotional well-being.

Aquarius (January 20 - February 18): Aquarius individuals are known for their innovative thinking and humanitarian nature. To maintain wellness, Aquarius should focus on activities that promote mental stimulation and social connection, such as volunteering or engaging in group activities. It's important for Aquarius to also prioritize self-care and relaxation to prevent emotional detachment.

Pisces (February 19 - March 20): Pisces individuals are known for their empathy and creativity. To maintain wellness, Pisces should focus on activities that promote emotional healing and self-expression, such as art therapy or journaling. It's important for Pisces to also practice grounding techniques and healthy boundaries to prevent emotional overwhelm.

By understanding the unique needs and tendencies associated with your zodiac sign, you can tailor your wellness practices to better support your overall health and well-being. Whether it's incorporating relaxation techniques for Aries or practicing self-compassion for Virgo, taking a personalized approach to wellness based on your zodiac sign can help you achieve balance and vitality in all areas of your life.

Holistic and Astrological Approaches to Health

In the realm of astrology, each zodiac sign is believed to govern specific parts of the body and influence overall health and well-being. By understanding the inherent qualities and tendencies associated with each sign, individuals can adopt holistic and astrological approaches to enhance their health and vitality.

Aries, the first sign of the zodiac, is associated with the head and face. Arians are known for their competitive spirit and high energy levels. To maintain optimal health, Aries individuals are advised to engage in physical activities that release pent-up energy and stress. Incorporating activities like martial arts, running, or yoga can help Aries natives channel their vitality in a positive way and prevent potential head-related issues.

Taurus governs the neck and throat in astrology. Taureans are known for their love of comfort and indulgence, which can sometimes lead to overeating or throat-related problems. To promote health, Taurus individuals can benefit from incorporating soothing practices like singing, chanting, or throat massages to maintain the health of their vocal cords and respiratory system.

Gemini, the sign of communication, rules the lungs and arms. Geminis are prone to mental restlessness and stress, which can impact their respiratory health. Engaging in activities that stimulate the mind and body, such as writing, painting, or playing a musical instrument, can help Geminis maintain mental and physical balance while supporting lung health.

Cancer governs the chest and stomach in astrology. Cancerians are known for their nurturing nature and emotional sensitivity. To support their well-being, Cancer individuals can benefit from practices that promote emotional release and digestive health. Activities like journaling, cooking nourishing meals, or practicing gentle yoga can help Cancerians maintain emotional balance and support their digestive system.

Leo rules the heart and back in astrology. Leos are known for their warmth and generosity, but they can also be prone to stress-related heart issues. To maintain heart health, Leos can benefit from activities that promote relaxation and self-expression, such as dancing, creative writing, or meditation. Strengthening the back through yoga or Pilates can also support overall spinal health for Leos.

Virgo governs the digestive system and nervous system in astrology. Virgos are known for their attention to detail and analytical nature. To support their health, Virgo individuals can benefit from practices that promote relaxation and digestive wellness, such as mindful eating, aromatherapy, or herbal remedies. Engaging in activities that stimulate the mind without causing undue stress can also benefit Virgos' nervous system.

Libra rules the kidneys and lower back in astrology. Librans are known for their sense of balance and harmony. To support their health, Libra individuals can benefit from practices that promote emotional equilibrium and kidney health, such as practicing mindfulness, maintaining healthy relationships, or engaging in activities that promote lower back strength and flexibility.

Scorpio governs the reproductive system and excretory organs in astrology. Scorpios are known for their intensity and emotional depth. To support their health, Scorpio individuals can benefit from practices that promote detoxification and emotional release, such as deep breathing exercises, meditation, or engaging in activities that promote sexual and reproductive health.

Sagittarius rules the hips and thighs in astrology. Sagittarians are known for their adventurous spirit and love of freedom. To support their health, Sagittarius individuals can benefit from activities that promote physical mobility and expansion, such as hiking, horseback riding, or practicing yoga. Maintaining flexibility and strength in the hips and thighs can support overall hip and lower body health for Sagittarians.

Capricorn governs the bones, joints, and skin in astrology. Capricorns are known for their ambition and discipline. To support their health, Capricorn individuals can benefit from practices that promote bone health and structural integrity, such as weight-bearing exercises, calcium-rich foods, or practicing good posture. Maintaining a consistent skincare routine and protecting the skin from harsh environmental factors can also support Capricorns' skin health.

Aquarius rules the circulatory system and ankles in astrology. Aquarians are known for their innovative thinking and humanitarian outlook. To support their health, Aquarius individuals can benefit from practices that promote circulation and ankle strength, such as aerobic exercise, cold water therapy, or wearing supportive footwear. Engaging in activities that promote social connection and community involvement can also benefit Aquarians' overall circulatory health.

Pisces governs the feet and lymphatic system in astrology. Pisceans are known for their intuitive nature and artistic talents. To support their health, Pisces individuals can benefit from practices that promote lymphatic drainage and emotional release, such as foot massages, reflexology, or engaging in creative pursuits. Maintaining healthy boundaries and engaging in activities that promote spiritual and emotional well-being can also support Pisceans' overall health and vitality.

By incorporating holistic and astrological approaches to health based on the qualities and tendencies associated with each zodiac sign, individuals can enhance their well-being and promote balance in mind, body, and spirit. Embracing these practices can lead to a deeper understanding of oneself and a harmonious integration of astrology into one's holistic wellness routine.

Chapter 17

Zodiac Signs in Daily Life

How Your Zodiac Sign Influences Your Daily Routine

Your zodiac sign can offer valuable insights into your personality traits, preferences, and tendencies, which in turn can influence your daily routine and how you navigate through life. Understanding how your zodiac sign impacts your daily life can help you optimize your habits, make better decisions, and enhance your overall well-being.

Each zodiac sign has its unique characteristics that shape the way individuals approach their daily routines. Aries, as the first sign of the zodiac, is known for its dynamic and energetic nature. Arians are often early risers, starting their day with vigor and enthusiasm. They thrive on challenges and are motivated by achieving their goals, making them proactive and goal-oriented in their daily tasks.

Taurus, on the other hand, appreciates stability and comfort in their routine. Taureans enjoy indulging in pleasurable activities like good food, relaxation, and physical comforts. They are known for their love of routine and may have a consistent schedule that brings them a sense of security and predictability.

Geminis are adaptable and curious individuals who thrive on variety and mental stimulation. Their daily routine may involve engaging in different activities, socializing with a diverse group of people, and constantly seeking new experiences to satisfy their curious minds.

Cancerians are nurturing and caring individuals who prioritize emotional well-being in their daily routine. They may spend time with loved ones, engage in self-care activities, and create a nurturing environment at home to feel emotionally secure and supported.

Leos are known for their confident and expressive nature, often incorporating creativity and passion into their daily routine. They may engage in activities that allow them to showcase their talents, seek attention and recognition, and find ways to express themselves authentically.

Virgos are detail-oriented and organized individuals who value efficiency and productivity in their daily tasks. They may have a structured routine that includes planning, organizing, and paying attention to the smallest details to ensure everything runs smoothly.

Libras, with their diplomatic and harmonious nature, may focus on creating balance and beauty in their daily routine. They may prioritize relationships, social interactions, and activities that promote peace and harmony in their environment.

Scorpios are intense and passionate individuals who may have a deep and transformative daily routine. They may engage in introspective activities, pursue their passions with determination, and seek emotional depth and authenticity in their interactions.

Sagittarians are adventurous and optimistic individuals who thrive on freedom and exploration in their daily routine. They may seek new experiences, travel to new places, and engage in activities that challenge their boundaries and expand their horizons.

Capricorns are ambitious and disciplined individuals who may have a structured and goal-oriented daily routine. They prioritize hard work, responsibility, and long-term success, often setting high standards for themselves and diligently working towards their goals.

Aquarians are innovative and independent individuals who may incorporate uniqueness and creativity into their daily routine. They may engage in unconventional activities, pursue their humanitarian values, and seek intellectual stimulation to fuel their progressive mindset.

Pisceans are sensitive and intuitive individuals who may have a dreamy and imaginative daily routine. They may engage in creative pursuits, connect with their emotions, and seek solitude and introspection to nurture their spiritual side.

Understanding how your zodiac sign influences your daily routine can help you align your habits and activities with your natural tendencies and preferences. By embracing the strengths and characteristics of your zodiac sign, you can create a fulfilling and balanced daily routine that supports your overall well-being and personal growth.

Navigating Challenges and Opportunities with Astrology

Astrology is a powerful tool that can help individuals understand themselves better and navigate life's challenges and opportunities. By exploring the influence of the planets and zodiac signs on our personalities and life paths, we can gain valuable insights into how to approach various situations and make the most of our strengths.

One of the key aspects of using astrology to navigate challenges is understanding our own strengths and weaknesses based on our zodiac sign. Each sign has its unique characteristics and tendencies that influence how we approach obstacles and opportunities. For example, Aries individuals are known for their bold and courageous nature, which can help them overcome challenges with confidence and determination. On the other hand, Taurus individuals are known for their patience and practicality, which can help them navigate difficulties with a steady and methodical approach.

Astrology can also provide guidance on how to leverage our strengths to overcome challenges and seize opportunities. By understanding the planetary influences in our birth chart, we can identify areas where we are naturally talented and where we may face obstacles. For instance, someone with a strong influence of Mars in their chart may excel in competitive situations but may also need to manage their impulsiveness. By being aware of these tendencies, individuals can proactively work on developing strategies to capitalize on their strengths and overcome potential pitfalls.

Furthermore, astrology can help us anticipate and prepare for upcoming challenges and opportunities. By studying planetary transits and aspects, we can gain insights into the cosmic energies at play and how they may impact our lives. For example, a challenging aspect between Saturn and Mercury may indicate a period of communication difficulties or mental blocks, while a harmonious aspect between Venus and Jupiter may signify a time of abundance and growth in relationships or finances.

In addition to providing insights into our own strengths and challenges, astrology can also offer valuable guidance on how to navigate relationships and interactions with others. By understanding the compatibility between different zodiac signs, we can improve our communication and understanding of others, leading to more harmonious relationships and collaborations. For example, knowing that a Leo individual values recognition and admiration can help us tailor our interactions with them to foster a positive and supportive relationship.

Overall, astrology is a versatile tool that can help us navigate life's challenges and opportunities with greater self-awareness and insight. By leveraging the wisdom of the stars, we can better understand ourselves, others, and the cosmic forces at play, empowering us to make informed decisions and embrace growth and transformation. Whether facing obstacles or seeking to capitalize on new opportunities, astrology can be a guiding light to help us navigate life's twists and turns with grace and wisdom.

Making the Most of Your Zodiac Sign's Strengths

Making the most of your zodiac sign's strengths is a fundamental aspect of harnessing your unique qualities and maximizing your potential in various aspects of life. Understanding and embracing the strengths associated with your zodiac sign can empower you to navigate challenges, make informed decisions, and lead a more fulfilling life.

Each zodiac sign possesses specific characteristics and traits that contribute to its strengths and abilities. By recognizing and leveraging these inherent qualities, individuals can enhance their personal growth, relationships, and overall well-being.

Aries, known as the pioneer of the zodiac, is characterized by traits such as courage, determination, and leadership. Those born under the sign of Aries can make the most of their strengths by embracing their boldness and taking risks to pursue their ambitions. By channeling their competitive spirit and passion into productive endeavors, Aries individuals can achieve success in their careers and relationships.

Taurus, the builder of the zodiac, is known for its stability, perseverance, and practicality. Taurus individuals can maximize their strengths by utilizing their strong work ethic and reliability to create a solid foundation for their goals. By staying grounded and focused on their objectives, Taurus individuals can achieve long-term success and financial security.

Gemini, the communicator of the zodiac, is characterized by traits such as intelligence, adaptability, and curiosity. Those born under the sign of Gemini can make the most of their strengths by leveraging their excellent communication skills and versatility. By engaging in intellectual pursuits and embracing new experiences, Gemini individuals can expand their horizons and forge meaningful connections with others.

Cancer, the nurturer of the zodiac, is known for its emotional depth, empathy, and intuition. Cancer individuals can maximize their strengths by cultivating their nurturing nature and forming deep emotional bonds with others. By tapping into their intuition and sensitivity, Cancer individuals can provide support and care for their loved ones while also prioritizing self-care and emotional well-being.

Leo, the leader of the zodiac, is characterized by traits such as confidence, creativity, and generosity. Those born under the sign of Leo can make the most of their strengths by embracing their natural charisma and creativity. By taking center stage and showcasing their talents, Leo individuals can inspire others and achieve recognition for their achievements.

Virgo, the analyst of the zodiac, is known for its attention to detail, organization, and practicality. Virgo individuals can maximize their strengths by utilizing their analytical skills and precision to excel in their endeavors. By maintaining a sense of order and efficiency in their daily routines, Virgo individuals can achieve success in their professional and personal lives.

Libra, the balancer of the zodiac, is characterized by traits such as diplomacy, harmony, and fairness. Those born under the sign of Libra can make the most of their strengths by fostering peace and balance in their relationships. By seeking harmony and compromise in their interactions with others, Libra individuals can cultivate strong partnerships and create a sense of equilibrium in their lives.

Scorpio, the transformer of the zodiac, is known for its intensity, passion, and resilience. Scorpio individuals can maximize their strengths by harnessing their inner strength and determination to overcome challenges. By embracing their transformative nature and diving deep into their emotions, Scorpio individuals can experience profound personal growth and empowerment.

Sagittarius, the explorer of the zodiac, is characterized by traits such as optimism, adventure, and independence. Those born under the sign of Sagittarius can make the most of their strengths by embracing their adventurous spirit and seeking new horizons. By pursuing their passions and exploring different cultures and philosophies, Sagittarius individuals can expand their worldview and embrace personal growth.

Capricorn, the achiever of the zodiac, is known for its ambition, discipline, and perseverance. Capricorn individuals can maximize their strengths by setting ambitious goals and working diligently to achieve them. By maintaining a strong sense of responsibility and commitment to their endeavors, Capricorn individuals can climb the ladder of success and realize their full potential.

Aquarius, the visionary of the zodiac, is characterized by traits such as innovation, independence, and humanitarianism. Those born under the sign of Aquarius can make the most of their strengths by embracing their unique perspective and progressive ideals. By championing social causes and embracing their individuality, Aquarius individuals can inspire change and make a positive impact on the world.

Pisces, the dreamer of the zodiac, is known for its sensitivity, creativity, and compassion. Pisces individuals can maximize their strengths by tapping into their artistic talents and intuitive abilities. By embracing their emotional depth and connecting with their inner selves, Pisces individuals can foster creativity and empathy in their relationships and pursuits.

In conclusion, making the most of your zodiac sign's strengths involves recognizing and embracing the unique qualities that define your astrological sign. By harnessing these inherent strengths and characteristics, individuals can navigate life's challenges, cultivate meaningful relationships, and pursue personal growth and fulfillment. Embracing your zodiac sign's strengths empowers you to lead a more authentic and purposeful life aligned with your true nature.

Chapter 18

Relationships and Compatibility

The Dynamics of Zodiac Sign Compatibility

Understanding zodiac sign compatibility is a fascinating aspect of astrology that can provide insight into the dynamics of relationships between individuals. Each zodiac sign is associated with specific personality traits, strengths, weaknesses, and characteristics that can influence how well two people may get along in various types of relationships. By exploring the compatibility between different zodiac signs, individuals can gain a deeper understanding of themselves and their connections with others.

Compatibility between zodiac signs is often determined by the elements and modalities that each sign belongs to. The four elements—Fire, Earth, Air, and Water—play a significant role in compatibility. Signs belonging to the same element tend to have a natural affinity for each other, as they share similar qualities and perspectives. For example, Fire signs (Aries, Leo, Sagittarius) are passionate, energetic, and adventurous, making them compatible with other Fire signs who appreciate their enthusiasm and drive.

The modalities—Cardinal, Fixed, and Mutable—also influence compatibility by highlighting how each sign approaches relationships and interacts with others. Cardinal signs (Aries, Cancer, Libra, Capricorn) are initiators and leaders, Fixed signs (Taurus, Leo, Scorpio, Aquarius) are stable and determined, and Mutable signs (Gemini, Virgo, Sagittarius, Pisces) are adaptable and flexible. Understanding the modalities can help individuals navigate the dynamics of their relationships and identify areas of strength and potential challenges.

In addition to elements and modalities, the positions of the Sun, Moon, and Rising signs in each individual's birth chart can provide valuable insights into compatibility. The Sun sign represents the core essence of a person's identity, the Moon sign reflects their emotional needs and responses, and the Rising sign influences their outward personality and first impressions. By considering all three signs in a relationship, individuals can gain a more comprehensive understanding of how they interact with each other on different levels.

When exploring zodiac sign compatibility, it is essential to remember that no relationship is perfect, and differences between signs can actually complement each other and lead to growth and balance. While some signs may naturally align more harmoniously due to shared elements or modalities, others may experience challenges that require compromise, communication, and understanding to overcome.

Ultimately, zodiac sign compatibility is a tool for self-awareness and personal growth in relationships. By recognizing the strengths and weaknesses of different signs and how they interact with each other, individuals can navigate their connections with greater empathy, insight, and harmony. Whether in love, friendship, or family relationships, understanding zodiac sign compatibility can deepen connections and foster mutual understanding and respect between individuals of different signs.

Love and Romance Compatibility

Love and Romance Compatibility is a fascinating aspect of astrology that explores how different zodiac signs interact and relate to each other in the realm of relationships. Understanding love and romance compatibility can provide valuable insights into the dynamics of a relationship, helping individuals navigate challenges and capitalize on opportunities for a fulfilling and harmonious connection.

In astrology, each zodiac sign possesses unique characteristics and personality traits that influence how they approach love and relationships. By examining the compatibility between two individuals' zodiac signs, astrologers can offer valuable insights into the potential strengths and challenges within a romantic partnership.

The compatibility between zodiac signs is often determined by the elements and modalities associated with each sign. The four elements - Fire, Earth, Air, and Water - play a significant role in understanding love compatibility. Signs belonging to the same element tend to have a natural affinity for each other, as they share similar values, motivations, and communication styles. For example, Fire signs (Aries, Leo, Sagittarius) are passionate and dynamic, while Earth signs (Taurus, Virgo, Capricorn) are grounded and practical. When Fire and Earth signs come together, they can complement each other's strengths and create a balanced and stable relationship.

Furthermore, the modalities of the zodiac signs - Cardinal, Fixed, and Mutable - also influence relationship dynamics. Cardinal signs (Aries, Cancer, Libra, Capricorn) are initiators and leaders, Fixed signs (Taurus, Leo, Scorpio, Aquarius) are determined and steadfast, and Mutable signs (Gemini, Virgo, Sagittarius, Pisces) are adaptable and flexible. Understanding how these modalities interact can shed light on how two individuals may navigate challenges and support each other in a relationship.

In love and romance compatibility, astrologers also consider the specific characteristics and traits of each zodiac sign. For example, Aries is known for being bold and adventurous, while Taurus values stability and security. When these two signs come together, Aries can inspire Taurus to step out of their comfort zone, while Taurus can provide grounding and stability for Aries.

Additionally, astrologers analyze the planetary placements in each individual's birth chart to provide more nuanced insights into love compatibility. The positions of Venus (the planet of love) and Mars (the planet of passion) in a person's chart can reveal their romantic preferences, desires, and approach to relationships. By comparing these placements between two individuals, astrologers can offer tailored advice on how to enhance harmony and understanding in their relationship.

Overall, love and romance compatibility in astrology offers a valuable framework for understanding the dynamics of romantic relationships. By exploring the elements, modalities, and specific traits of each zodiac sign, individuals can gain a deeper appreciation for their partner's unique qualities and strengths. Whether seeking to strengthen an existing relationship or explore new romantic connections, astrology can provide valuable insights and guidance for cultivating fulfilling and harmonious love connections.

Friendship and Family Compatibility

Understanding how each zodiac sign interacts with others is crucial in fostering harmonious relationships, whether in friendships or within families. Astrology provides insights into the dynamics between different signs, highlighting areas of compatibility and potential challenges. By delving into the unique traits and energies of each zodiac sign, individuals can better navigate their social interactions and strengthen their bonds with others.

Friendship Compatibility:
Friendship compatibility is determined by how well two individuals' personalities complement each other. Some signs naturally gravitate towards each other, forming deep and lasting friendships, while others may struggle to find common ground.

Aries, for example, is known for their adventurous and dynamic nature, making them great friends with fellow fire signs like Leo and Sagittarius who share their enthusiasm for life. On the other hand, they may clash with more grounded earth signs like Taurus or Capricorn due to their differing approaches to life.

Taurus, with their loyal and steady demeanor, values stability in their friendships. They often form strong bonds with water signs like Cancer and Pisces, who provide emotional support and understanding. However, they may find it challenging to connect with the independent and unpredictable nature of air signs like Gemini or Aquarius.

Gemini, the social butterfly of the zodiac, can easily adapt to different social circles and make friends from all walks of life. Their witty and communicative nature resonates well with fellow air signs like Libra and Aquarius, fostering intellectually stimulating friendships. However, they may struggle with the emotional depth required in friendships with water signs like Scorpio or Pisces.

Family Compatibility:
Family dynamics play a significant role in shaping individuals' identities and values. Understanding how each zodiac sign interacts within the family unit can help improve communication and foster stronger bonds among family members.

Cancer, the nurturing and empathetic sign, thrives in familial settings where emotional connections are valued. They often play the role of the caregiver within the family, offering unconditional love and support to their loved ones. Cancer individuals form deep bonds with water signs like Scorpio and Pisces, creating a harmonious and emotionally fulfilling family environment.

Leo, the charismatic and expressive sign, brings warmth and vitality to the family dynamic. They enjoy being the center of attention and thrive in environments where they are appreciated for their unique qualities. Leos may clash with other strong-willed signs like Aries or Capricorn, but they can create a loving and supportive family unit with fire signs like Sagittarius and Aries.

Virgo, the practical and detail-oriented sign, values organization and efficiency within the family setting. They excel in roles that require attention to detail and problem-solving skills, often taking on the responsibility of managing household tasks. Virgos may find common ground with earth signs like Taurus and Capricorn, who share their practical approach to life, but may struggle with the emotional intensity of water signs like Scorpio or Pisces.

By exploring friendship and family compatibility through the lens of astrology, individuals can gain valuable insights into their relationships with others and work towards building stronger and more fulfilling connections in their social and familial circles.

Working with Different Zodiac Signs

Understanding the dynamics of working with different zodiac signs can greatly enhance your interpersonal relationships, whether in the workplace or in your personal life. Each zodiac sign has its unique characteristics, strengths, weaknesses, and communication styles that can influence how they approach tasks, collaborate with others, and handle challenges. By recognizing and appreciating these differences, you can create more harmonious and productive interactions with individuals of various zodiac signs.

Aries individuals are known for their leadership qualities, assertiveness, and competitive nature. When working with an Aries, it is important to provide them with opportunities to take charge and showcase their initiative. They thrive in environments that allow them to set goals, take risks, and lead projects. To effectively collaborate with an Aries, offer them challenges that stimulate their creativity and passion for success.

Taurus individuals are dependable, practical, and methodical in their approach to work. They excel in tasks that require attention to detail, patience, and perseverance. When working with a Taurus, provide them with clear instructions, structure, and stability. They appreciate consistency and prefer to work at a steady pace towards tangible goals. Recognize their hard work and dedication to motivate them to excel further.

Gemini individuals are versatile, communicative, and adaptable to change. They thrive in fast-paced environments that stimulate their curiosity and intellect. When working with a Gemini, engage them in open discussions, brainstorming sessions, and diverse projects that challenge their versatility.

They enjoy learning new skills, networking with others, and exploring innovative ideas. Keep them mentally stimulated to harness their full potential.

Cancer individuals are nurturing, intuitive, and empathetic towards others. They excel in roles that involve caregiving, emotional support, and building strong relationships. When working with a Cancer, create a supportive and collaborative atmosphere where they can express their feelings and connect with their colleagues on a personal level. Show appreciation for their sensitivity and dedication to foster a harmonious work environment.

Leo individuals are confident, charismatic, and ambitious in their pursuits. They thrive in roles that allow them to shine, lead teams, and showcase their creativity. When working with a Leo, acknowledge their strengths, provide them with opportunities for recognition, and encourage their leadership skills. They appreciate projects that allow them to express their individuality and make a significant impact.

Virgo individuals are analytical, detail-oriented, and organized in their approach to work. They excel in tasks that require precision, critical thinking, and problem-solving skills. When working with a Virgo, provide them with clear expectations, constructive feedback, and logical reasoning. They appreciate efficiency, structure, and attention to detail in their work environment. Encourage their dedication to quality and accuracy to achieve optimal results.

Libra individuals are diplomatic, sociable, and cooperative in their interactions with others. They excel in roles that involve teamwork, negotiation, and conflict resolution. When working with a Libra, foster a harmonious and inclusive environment where they can collaborate with others, promote fairness, and seek consensus. They appreciate opportunities to create balance, harmony, and mutual understanding among team members.

Scorpio individuals are intense, passionate, and resourceful in their pursuits. They excel in roles that require depth, focus, and determination. When working with a Scorpio, respect their privacy, trust their instincts, and allow them to delve into complex tasks that challenge their investigative skills. They appreciate honesty, loyalty, and authenticity in their relationships. Support their transformative journey to unlock their full potential.

Sagittarius individuals are adventurous, optimistic, and philosophical in their outlook on life. They excel in roles that involve exploration, learning, and broadening their horizons. When working with a Sagittarius, encourage their enthusiasm, provide them with opportunities for growth, and embrace their love for freedom and independence. They appreciate flexibility, open-mindedness, and a sense of humor in their work environment. Inspire their quest for knowledge and wisdom to fuel their personal and professional development.

Capricorn individuals are disciplined, ambitious, and practical in their approach to work. They excel in roles that require structure, planning, and perseverance. When working with a Capricorn, respect their work ethic, acknowledge their achievements, and provide them with clear goals to strive towards. They appreciate professionalism, reliability, and consistency in their work environment. Support their long-term goals and aspirations to help them achieve success.

Aquarius individuals are innovative, independent, and humanitarian in their endeavors. They excel in roles that involve creativity, originality, and social change. When working with an Aquarius, encourage their unconventional ideas, support their vision for the future, and embrace their unique perspective on solving problems. They appreciate freedom, diversity, and inclusivity in their work environment. Empower their creativity and individuality to make a positive impact on society.

Pisces individuals are compassionate, imaginative, and intuitive in their interactions with others. They excel in roles that involve creativity, empathy, and spiritual growth. When working with a Pisces, nurture their emotional sensitivity, inspire their artistic talents, and provide them with opportunities to connect with their intuition. They appreciate empathy, kindness, and understanding in their relationships. Encourage their dreams and aspirations to help them achieve emotional fulfillment and personal growth.

In conclusion, working with individuals of different zodiac signs requires understanding, adaptability, and appreciation for their unique qualities and characteristics. By recognizing the strengths and weaknesses of each zodiac sign, you can foster positive relationships, effective communication, and productive collaborations in various aspects of your life. Embrace the diversity and richness of the zodiac signs to create a harmonious and fulfilling environment for personal and professional growth.

Chapter 19

Career and Success

How Your Zodiac Sign Affects Your Career Choices

Your zodiac sign can offer valuable insights into your personality traits, strengths, weaknesses, and inclinations, which in turn can influence the career paths you are naturally drawn to and excel in. Understanding how your zodiac sign impacts your career choices can help you make informed decisions about your professional life and find fulfillment in your chosen field.

Aries: The Pioneer

Aries individuals are known for their boldness, leadership skills, and competitive nature. They thrive in dynamic and challenging environments where they can take initiative and drive projects forward. Careers that align with Aries traits include entrepreneurship, sales, marketing, and any role that requires quick decision-making and a go-getter attitude.

Taurus: The Builder

Taurus individuals are reliable, hardworking, and practical. They excel in roles that require patience, determination, and a steady work ethic. Careers in finance, real estate, agriculture, or any field that values stability and tangible results are well-suited for Taureans.

Gemini: The Communicator

Geminis are versatile, witty, and intellectually curious. They thrive in roles that involve communication, networking, and mental agility. Careers in journalism, public relations, teaching, or any field that allows them to use their communication skills and adaptability are ideal for Geminis.

Cancer: The Nurturer

Cancer individuals are empathetic, intuitive, and nurturing. They excel in roles that involve caregiving, counseling, or working with emotions. Careers in healthcare, social work, education, or any field that allows them to support and nurture others are fulfilling for Cancerians.

Leo: The Leader

Leos are confident, charismatic, and ambitious. They shine in leadership roles and enjoy being in the spotlight. Careers in entertainment, management, performing arts, or any field that allows them to showcase their creativity and charisma are well-suited for Leos.

Virgo: The Analyst
Virgos are detail-oriented, analytical, and perfectionists. They excel in roles that require precision, organization, and problem-solving skills. Careers in research, data analysis, healthcare, or any field that values meticulous attention to detail are ideal for Virgos.

Libra: The Balancer
Libras are diplomatic, harmonious, and sociable. They thrive in roles that involve negotiation, mediation, and maintaining balance. Careers in law, diplomacy, fashion, or any field that requires a sense of fairness and diplomacy are well-suited for Librans.

Scorpio: The Transformer
Scorpios are passionate, intense, and strategic. They excel in roles that involve deep analysis, investigation, and transformation. Careers in psychology, detective work, research, or any field that requires probing beneath the surface are fulfilling for Scorpios.

Sagittarius: The Explorer
Sagittarians are adventurous, optimistic, and philosophical. They thrive in roles that involve travel, learning, and exploring new horizons. Careers in education, travel industry, publishing, or any field that allows them to expand their horizons and seek new experiences are ideal for Sagittarians.

Capricorn: The Achiever
Capricorns are disciplined, ambitious, and focused on long-term goals. They excel in roles that require hard work, perseverance, and strategic planning. Careers in finance, business management, engineering, or any field that values determination and ambition are well-suited for Capricorns.

Aquarius: The Visionary
Aquarians are innovative, independent, and humanitarian. They shine in roles that involve cutting-edge technology, social change, and unconventional thinking. Careers in technology, social activism, research, or any field that allows them to think outside the box and make a difference in society are fulfilling for Aquarians.

Pisces: The Dreamer

Pisceans are creative, intuitive, and empathetic. They excel in roles that involve imagination, spirituality, and emotional connection. Careers in the arts, healing professions, charity work, or any field that allows them to tap into their intuition and compassion are ideal for Pisceans.

In conclusion, your zodiac sign can provide valuable insights into your natural talents, preferences, and inclinations when it comes to career choices. By understanding how your zodiac sign influences your professional life, you can make informed decisions that align with your strengths and values, leading to a more fulfilling and successful career path.

Strategies for Career Success Based on Your Zodiac Sign

Understanding your zodiac sign can offer valuable insights into the best strategies for achieving success in your career. Each zodiac sign possesses unique characteristics and traits that can influence how individuals approach their professional lives. By leveraging the strengths associated with your sign and being mindful of potential weaknesses, you can develop a tailored approach to career success. Below are some strategies for career success based on each zodiac sign:

1. Aries (March 21 - April 19):

Aries individuals are known for their leadership qualities and competitive nature. To excel in their careers, Aries should focus on taking on challenging projects that allow them to showcase their initiative and drive. Setting clear goals and staying focused on their objectives will help Aries navigate their career path successfully.

2. Taurus (April 20 - May 20):

Taurus individuals are reliable and hardworking, making them valuable assets in any workplace. To achieve career success, Taurus should prioritize stability and consistency in their professional endeavors. Building a strong work ethic and demonstrating their practical skills will help Taurus advance in their chosen field.

3. Gemini (May 21 - June 20):

Geminis are versatile and adaptable, making them well-suited for diverse career paths. To succeed in their careers, Geminis should focus on developing their communication skills and fostering connections with others. Embracing change and seeking out opportunities for growth will enable Geminis to thrive in their professional lives.

4. Cancer (June 21 - July 22):

Cancer individuals are nurturing and empathetic, making them well-suited for roles that involve caring for others. To achieve career success, Cancers should prioritize emotional intelligence and cultivate strong relationships with colleagues. Leveraging their intuition and sensitivity will help Cancers excel in professions that require a compassionate touch.

5. Leo (July 23 - August 22):

Leos are confident and ambitious, with a natural flair for leadership. To succeed in their careers, Leos should focus on showcasing their creativity and charisma. Taking on roles that allow them to shine and seeking opportunities for recognition will enable Leos to reach their full potential in their chosen field.

6. Virgo (August 23 - September 22):

Virgos are detail-oriented and analytical, making them well-suited for roles that require precision and organization. To excel in their careers, Virgos should focus on honing their problem-solving skills and attention to detail. Setting high standards for themselves and seeking out opportunities for growth will help Virgos achieve success in their professional lives.

7. Libra (September 23 - October 22):

Libras are diplomatic and sociable, with a natural talent for bringing harmony to their surroundings. To succeed in their careers, Libras should focus on building strong partnerships and fostering collaboration with others. Balancing their desire for fairness and justice with their need for creativity will help Libras thrive in their chosen profession.

8. Scorpio (October 23 - November 21):

Scorpios are determined and resourceful, with a keen intuition that serves them well in their careers. To achieve success, Scorpios should focus on harnessing their power and resilience. Embracing challenges and staying true to their passions will enable Scorpios to overcome obstacles and achieve their professional goals.

9. Sagittarius (November 22 - December 21):

Sagittarians are adventurous and optimistic, with a thirst for knowledge and new experiences. To succeed in their careers, Sagittarians should focus on expanding their horizons and seeking out opportunities for growth. Embracing change and staying open to new possibilities will help Sagittarians thrive in their chosen field.

10. Capricorn (December 22 - January 19):

Capricorns are ambitious and disciplined, with a strong sense of responsibility and determination. To achieve career success, Capricorns should focus on setting clear goals and working diligently toward achieving them. Demonstrating their leadership skills and commitment to excellence will help Capricorns advance in their professional endeavors.

11. Aquarius (January 20 - February 18):

Aquarians are innovative and independent, with a unique perspective that sets them apart in their careers. To succeed, Aquarians should focus on embracing their individuality and thinking outside the box. Seeking out opportunities for creativity and originality will help Aquarians make a meaningful impact in their chosen field.

12. Pisces (February 19 - March 20):

Pisceans are intuitive and compassionate, with a deep empathy for others. To achieve career success, Pisces should focus on tapping into their creativity and imagination. Embracing their sensitivity and using it to connect with others will help Pisces excel in professions that require a caring and empathetic touch.

By understanding the strengths and weaknesses associated with your zodiac sign, you can develop tailored strategies for achieving success in your career. Leveraging your unique traits and characteristics can help you navigate challenges, seize opportunities, and ultimately reach your full potential in the professional world.

Finding Fulfillment and Balance in Your Professional Life

Finding fulfillment and balance in your professional life is crucial for overall well-being and satisfaction. Understanding how your zodiac sign influences your career choices and strategies can help you navigate your professional journey with more clarity and purpose.

Each zodiac sign has unique characteristics and tendencies that can impact career choices and success. For example, Aries individuals are known for their leadership qualities and thrive in roles that allow them to take charge and initiate new projects. Taurus individuals, on the other hand, excel in roles that require stability, reliability, and a methodical approach to work.

When it comes to finding fulfillment in your career, it is important to align your professional goals with your inherent strengths and interests. For instance, Geminis, being natural communicators, may find satisfaction in roles that involve networking, public speaking, or writing. Cancer individuals, with their nurturing and empathetic nature, may excel in caregiving professions or roles that involve supporting others.

Understanding your strengths and weaknesses based on your zodiac sign can help you make informed career choices and set realistic goals for professional growth. Leos, known for their confidence and charisma, may thrive in roles that allow them to showcase their creativity and leadership skills. Virgos, with their attention to detail and analytical abilities, may excel in roles that require precision and problem-solving.

Achieving balance in your professional life involves recognizing your limitations and taking steps to address them. For example, Libras, who value harmony and collaboration, may need to work on asserting themselves in competitive environments to achieve career success. Scorpios, with their intense and passionate nature, may need to find ways to manage stress and avoid burnout in high-pressure work settings.

Building strong relationships with colleagues and mentors can also contribute to your professional fulfillment and success. Sagittarius individuals, known for their adventurous spirit and love for learning, may benefit from seeking mentors who can guide them in their career development and provide valuable insights. Capricorns, with their ambition and determination, may thrive in environments that offer opportunities for growth and advancement. Incorporating holistic and astrological approaches to career planning can help you achieve a sense of balance and fulfillment in your professional life. Aquarius individuals, with their innovative and visionary mindset, may benefit from exploring unconventional career paths or pursuing entrepreneurial ventures. Pisces individuals, known for their creativity and intuition, may find fulfillment in roles that allow them to express their artistic talents and make a positive impact on others.

By leveraging your strengths, addressing your weaknesses, and aligning your career goals with your zodiac sign's characteristics, you can find fulfillment and balance in your professional life. Remember to stay true to yourself, pursue opportunities that resonate with your passions and values, and embrace challenges as opportunities for growth and development.

Chapter 20

Zodiac Signs and Personal Growth

Using Astrology for Personal Development

Astrology has been used for centuries as a tool for self-discovery, personal growth, and understanding one's strengths and weaknesses. By exploring your zodiac sign and birth chart, you can gain valuable insights into your personality, motivations, and potential areas for growth. Here, we delve into how you can harness the power of astrology for personal development.

1. Self-awareness: Astrology offers a unique lens through which to gain self-awareness. By understanding the traits associated with your zodiac sign, as well as the influence of your moon and rising signs, you can uncover hidden aspects of your personality. This self-awareness can help you identify patterns of behavior, triggers for certain emotions, and areas where you may need to focus on personal growth.

2. Setting goals: Astrology can be a powerful tool for setting goals and intentions. By aligning your goals with the strengths and qualities of your zodiac sign, you can work towards achieving them in a way that feels authentic and aligned with your true self. For example, a fiery Aries may thrive on setting ambitious and challenging goals, while a practical Taurus may benefit from setting concrete and achievable milestones.

3. Understanding challenges: Astrology can also shed light on the challenges and obstacles you may face in your personal growth journey. By examining the aspects in your birth chart that indicate areas of difficulty or potential roadblocks, you can proactively address these challenges and develop strategies for overcoming them. For instance, a sensitive Cancer may struggle with setting boundaries, while a perfectionistic Virgo may need to work on letting go of control.

4. Embracing your full potential: Astrology can help you embrace your full potential by highlighting your unique strengths and talents. By recognizing and nurturing these qualities, you can cultivate a sense of empowerment and confidence in pursuing your dreams and aspirations. Whether you are a creative and intuitive Pisces or a determined and ambitious Capricorn, astrology can guide you towards fulfilling your highest potential.

5. Personal growth practices: Astrology can complement traditional personal growth practices such as meditation, journaling, and therapy. By incorporating astrological insights into your self-care routine, you can deepen your understanding of yourself and your inner world. For example, meditating on the qualities of your sun sign can help you cultivate self-acceptance and self-love, while journaling about the influence of your moon sign can enhance emotional awareness and processing.

In conclusion, astrology offers a rich and multifaceted approach to personal development. By leveraging the wisdom of the stars, you can gain a deeper understanding of yourself, set meaningful goals, navigate challenges, embrace your strengths, and embark on a journey of self-discovery and growth. Whether you are just beginning your astrological journey or have been studying the stars for years, incorporating astrology into your personal development practice can lead to profound insights and transformative experiences.

Setting Goals and Achieving Growth with Astrological Guidance

Setting goals and achieving growth with astrological guidance can be a powerful tool for personal development and self-awareness. By understanding your zodiac sign and how it influences your strengths, weaknesses, and tendencies, you can tailor your goals and strategies for growth to align with your astrological profile.

Each zodiac sign has unique characteristics and traits that can impact how you approach goal-setting and personal growth. For example, Aries individuals are known for their ambitious and competitive nature, making them well-suited for setting challenging goals and pushing themselves to achieve them. Taurus individuals, on the other hand, are known for their patience and determination, making them excellent at setting long-term goals and staying focused on achieving them.

When using astrological guidance to set goals, it is important to consider not only your sun sign but also your moon sign and rising sign. Your sun sign represents your core identity and motivations, while your moon sign reflects your emotional needs and inner world. Your rising sign, or ascendant, influences how you present yourself to the world and can provide valuable insights into your strengths and challenges.

To effectively set goals using astrological guidance, start by identifying areas of your life where you want to grow or make changes. Consider your zodiac sign's strengths and weaknesses and how they may impact your ability to achieve these goals. For example, if you are a Gemini who struggles with indecision, setting clear and specific goals can help you stay focused and motivated.

Next, align your goals with the natural tendencies and talents associated with your zodiac sign. For instance, if you are a Cancer who values emotional connections and nurturing relationships, setting goals that involve building stronger bonds with loved ones or creating a supportive home environment can be particularly fulfilling and motivating for you.

In addition to setting goals that align with your zodiac sign, consider incorporating astrological insights into your goal-setting process. For example, pay attention to planetary transits and alignments that may influence your energy levels, motivation, and opportunities for growth. By timing your goal-setting and actions to coincide with favorable astrological influences, you can maximize your chances of success and growth.

It is also important to be flexible and adaptable in your goal-setting approach, as astrological influences are constantly changing. As you progress towards your goals, regularly check in with your astrological chart and seek guidance from an astrologer to adjust your strategies and stay aligned with the cosmic energies at play.

Overall, setting goals and achieving growth with astrological guidance can be a transformative and empowering process. By harnessing the wisdom of the stars and aligning your goals with your astrological profile, you can unlock your full potential, overcome obstacles, and create a life that reflects your true essence and aspirations.

Embracing Your Full Potential Through Understanding Your Zodiac Sign

Understanding your zodiac sign is not just about knowing your strengths and weaknesses; it is also about recognizing your unique qualities and harnessing them to reach your full potential. Each zodiac sign has its own set of characteristics and traits that can guide you towards personal growth and self-improvement. By delving deeper into the essence of your zodiac sign, you can uncover hidden talents, address areas of improvement, and embrace a more fulfilling life journey.

One key aspect of embracing your full potential through understanding your zodiac sign is self-awareness. By knowing your zodiac sign's personality traits, strengths, and weaknesses, you can gain a deeper understanding of yourself. This self-awareness allows you to make conscious decisions that align with your true nature and values. For example, if you are a fiery Aries, known for their boldness and leadership skills, embracing these traits can help you take charge of your life and pursue your ambitions with confidence.

Moreover, understanding your zodiac sign can also provide insights into your relationships with others. By knowing the compatibility between your zodiac sign and those of your loved ones, you can navigate interpersonal dynamics more effectively. For instance, a sensitive Cancer may find harmony with a supportive Taurus, while a free-spirited Sagittarius may clash with a practical Virgo. By recognizing these dynamics, you can cultivate stronger connections and foster healthier relationships.

Furthermore, embracing your full potential through your zodiac sign involves setting goals and aspirations that align with your astrological profile. Each zodiac sign has its own set of career preferences, communication styles, and approaches to success. By leveraging this knowledge, you can tailor your goals and ambitions to suit your inherent strengths and inclinations. For instance, a detail-oriented Virgo may excel in analytical roles, while a creative Pisces may thrive in artistic pursuits.

Additionally, embracing your zodiac sign can also lead to personal growth and development. By embracing the positive traits of your zodiac sign and working on improving your weaknesses, you can embark on a journey of self-improvement and self-discovery. For example, a stubborn Taurus can work on being more adaptable and open-minded, while an indecisive Libra can cultivate decisiveness and assertiveness.

In conclusion, embracing your full potential through understanding your zodiac sign is a transformative journey towards self-discovery and self-realization. By delving into the depths of your astrological profile, you can unlock hidden potentials, improve upon your weaknesses, and lead a more purposeful and fulfilling life. Embrace the wisdom of the stars, and let your zodiac sign guide you towards embracing your true self and reaching your highest potential.

Chapter 21

Advanced Astrological Concepts

The Role of Retrogrades in Astrology

Retrogrades in astrology play a significant role in understanding the energetic shifts and challenges that individuals may experience during certain periods. When a planet goes into retrograde motion, it appears to move backward in its orbit from the perspective of Earth. This phenomenon has been observed since ancient times and is believed to influence various aspects of life, including personal growth, relationships, and communication.

Each planet in the solar system can go into retrograde, with Mercury being the most well-known retrograde due to its frequency. During Mercury retrograde, which occurs about three to four times a year, communication may become disrupted, leading to misunderstandings, technological glitches, and delays in travel and decision-making. However, Mercury retrograde is also a time for reflection, revision, and reevaluation of plans and projects.

Other planets, such as Venus, Mars, Jupiter, Saturn, Uranus, Neptune, and Pluto, also go into retrograde motion periodically, each bringing its unique influence. For example, Venus retrograde may bring up issues related to love, relationships, and self-worth, prompting individuals to reassess their values and priorities in these areas. Mars retrograde can affect energy levels, motivation, and assertiveness, leading to potential conflicts or delays in pursuing goals.

Saturn retrograde can bring a sense of introspection and accountability, urging individuals to take responsibility for their actions and make necessary adjustments for long-term success. Uranus retrograde may trigger unexpected changes or revelations that shake up the status quo, encouraging innovation and breaking free from limiting patterns. Neptune retrograde can enhance spiritual insights and intuition while also highlighting illusions or delusions that need to be addressed.

Pluto retrograde delves into deep transformation and regeneration, urging individuals to confront their fears, insecurities, and power dynamics in order to emerge stronger and more empowered. These retrograde periods offer opportunities for inner work, introspection, and growth, allowing individuals to shed old patterns, beliefs, and behaviors that no longer serve their highest good.

Understanding the role of retrogrades in astrology involves recognizing their cyclical nature and the lessons they bring during their retrograde phases. By paying attention to the planetary energies at play and how they interact with individual natal charts, astrologers and enthusiasts can gain deeper insights into the cosmic influences shaping their lives.

In conclusion, retrogrades in astrology are not to be feared but rather embraced as opportunities for growth, reflection, and transformation. By acknowledging and working with the energies of retrograde planets, individuals can navigate challenges with greater awareness and resilience, ultimately leading to personal evolution and self-discovery.

Eclipses and Their Impact on the Zodiac

Eclipses are powerful astronomical events that have significant impacts on the zodiac signs and astrology as a whole. In astrology, eclipses are considered pivotal moments that can bring about change, transformation, and revelations in our lives. Understanding the effects of eclipses can provide valuable insights into how they influence the energies and dynamics of the zodiac signs.

There are two types of eclipses: solar eclipses and lunar eclipses. Solar eclipses occur during a new moon when the moon passes between the Earth and the sun, blocking the sun's light and creating a shadow on the Earth. In astrology, solar eclipses are associated with beginnings, new opportunities, and external events that propel us towards growth and evolution. Solar eclipses are potent times for setting intentions, starting new projects, and making important decisions that can shape our future.

On the other hand, lunar eclipses occur during a full moon when the Earth passes between the sun and the moon, casting a shadow on the moon. In astrology, lunar eclipses are linked to endings, closures, and internal shifts that prompt us to release what no longer serves us. Lunar eclipses are times for reflection, emotional healing, and letting go of the past in order to make space for new growth and transformation.

In terms of their impact on the zodiac signs, eclipses can activate specific areas of our lives based on where they fall in our birth charts. The zodiac sign and house in which an eclipse occurs can provide clues about the themes and areas of life that will be highlighted during that time. For example, a solar eclipse in Aries may emphasize themes of self-discovery, independence, and personal identity, while a lunar eclipse in Cancer could bring focus to emotions, family dynamics, and nurturing relationships.

Eclipses also have a collective influence on the zodiac signs, affecting global events, societal trends, and collective consciousness. Astrologers often track eclipses to observe patterns and correlations between celestial events and worldly phenomena. Eclipses can act as catalysts for change on a larger scale, triggering shifts in political landscapes, cultural movements, and environmental conditions.

During eclipse seasons, which occur approximately twice a year, the energies of change and transformation are heightened, creating a potent period for personal growth and evolution. It is important for individuals to pay attention to the messages and lessons that eclipses bring, as they can offer valuable insights and opportunities for self-awareness and empowerment.

In conclusion, eclipses play a significant role in astrology and the zodiac signs by highlighting key themes of change, transformation, and growth. By understanding the impact of eclipses on our lives and the zodiac signs, we can navigate these powerful celestial events with awareness, intention, and readiness to embrace the shifts they bring.

Understanding and Interpreting Transits

Transits in astrology refer to the current positions of the planets in relation to an individual's natal (birth) chart. These planetary transits play a significant role in shaping and influencing a person's life experiences, events, and overall growth. Understanding and interpreting transits can provide valuable insights into the energies at play and the potential opportunities or challenges that may arise.

Transits are a dynamic and ever-changing phenomenon, as the planets continuously move through the zodiac, forming different aspects with each other and with the positions of planets in an individual's natal chart. By tracking these transits and understanding their symbolism, astrologers can offer guidance on how to navigate and make the most of the energies present in a person's life at any given time.

One of the key concepts in interpreting transits is the idea of planetary aspects. As planets move through the zodiac, they form aspects with each other, such as conjunctions, squares, trines, and oppositions. These aspects create different energies and influences that can manifest in various areas of life. For example, a conjunction between Jupiter and Venus may bring opportunities for love, abundance, and growth, while a square between Mars and Saturn could indicate challenges, conflicts, or obstacles that need to be overcome.

Another important factor to consider when interpreting transits is the house placement of the transiting planets in relation to the natal chart. Each house in the natal chart represents different areas of life, such as career, relationships, health, and spirituality. When a planet transits a particular house, it activates and energizes that area, bringing its themes to the forefront of a person's experience. For instance, if transiting Saturn enters the 7th house of partnerships, it may signal a period of increased focus on relationships, commitment, and responsibilities in that area of life.

Astrologers also pay attention to the speed of the transiting planets, as faster-moving planets like Mercury and Venus tend to bring more fleeting influences, while slower-moving planets such as Saturn and Pluto signify longer-term developments and transformations. The timing of transits is crucial in understanding when certain energies will be most prominent and when they may start to wane.

Interpreting transits involves a blend of intuition, knowledge of astrological symbolism, and an understanding of the individual's unique natal chart. By studying the interactions between the transiting planets and the natal positions, astrologers can provide valuable insights into the timing of events, opportunities for growth, and challenges that may arise during a particular transit period.

In conclusion, understanding and interpreting transits is a valuable tool in astrology for gaining deeper insights into the energies at play in a person's life and for navigating the ebbs and flows of cosmic influences. By paying attention to planetary aspects, house placements, and the timing of transits, individuals can better prepare themselves to make informed decisions, seize opportunities for growth, and navigate challenges with greater awareness and clarity.

Chapter 22

Putting It All Together: A Comprehensive Guide

How to Read and Interpret Your Birth Chart

Reading and interpreting your birth chart is a fascinating and insightful way to gain a deeper understanding of yourself and your life's path. A birth chart, also known as a natal chart, is a snapshot of the sky at the exact moment of your birth and serves as a personalized map of the celestial bodies' positions in relation to the zodiac signs and houses. Here's a detailed guide on how to read and interpret your birth chart:

1. Gather Your Birth Information: To create your birth chart, you'll need your birth date, time, and place. The accuracy of the birth time is crucial as it determines the positions of the planets in the houses of your chart.

2. Understand the Components of Your Birth Chart:
   - **Planets:** Each planet represents different aspects of your personality and life. For example, Mercury governs communication and intellect, while Venus rules love and relationships.
   - **Zodiac Signs:** The zodiac signs the planets are placed in influence how their energies are expressed. For instance, a Moon in Aries may indicate emotional impulsiveness.
   - **Houses:** The houses in your birth chart represent different areas of life, such as career, relationships, and home life. The placement of planets in houses shows where these energies manifest in your life.

3. Identify the Key Points in Your Chart:
   - **Sun Sign:** Your Sun sign represents your core identity and the traits you express outwardly.
   - **Moon Sign:** Your Moon sign reveals your emotional needs and inner self.
   - **Rising Sign (Ascendant):** The Rising sign governs how you present yourself to the world and your initial reactions.
   - **Aspects:** Pay attention to the angles (aspects) formed between planets, which indicate how they interact and influence each other.

4. Analyze Planetary Placements:
   - **Stelliums:** If three or more planets are clustered in one sign or house, it indicates a strong emphasis on that area of life.
   - **Retrogrades:** Planets in retrograde motion suggest internalized energy or areas for reflection and growth.

5. Consider the Elements and Modalities:
   - **Elements:** The distribution of planets in the elements (fire, earth, air, water) reveals your elemental balance and predominant energies.
   - **Modalities:** The modalities (cardinal, fixed, mutable) show how you approach change and adapt to circumstances.

6. Consult Resources and Seek Interpretations:
   - Utilize astrology books, online resources, or consult with a professional astrologer to deepen your understanding of your birth chart.
   - Keep in mind that astrology is a tool for self-awareness and personal growth, not a deterministic prediction of your future.

By delving into the intricacies of your birth chart, you can uncover hidden potentials, understand your motivations and challenges, and navigate life's complexities with greater clarity and self-awareness. Embrace the insights offered by astrology as a means to empower yourself and cultivate personal growth and fulfillment.

Combining Sun, Moon, and Rising Signs

Combining Sun, Moon, and Rising Signs is a crucial aspect of understanding one's astrological profile and gaining deeper insights into one's personality, emotions, and overall life path. Each of these elements represents different facets of an individual's being, and by analyzing them together, a comprehensive and nuanced understanding of a person's astrological makeup can be achieved.

The Sun Sign, often the most well-known and recognized aspect of astrology, represents the core essence of an individual's personality. It signifies one's ego, basic identity, and the traits that are most visible to the outside world. The Sun Sign reflects how a person expresses themselves, their natural inclinations, and their overall life purpose. For example, a person with a Sun in Leo may exhibit qualities of creativity, leadership, and a strong sense of self-expression.

The Moon Sign, on the other hand, represents one's inner emotional world, instincts, and subconscious mind. It reveals how a person processes emotions, their deepest needs, and their intuitive responses to situations. Understanding the Moon Sign can provide insights into one's emotional reactions, inner motivations, and how they nurture themselves and others. For instance, an individual with a Moon in Pisces may be highly empathetic, creative, and attuned to the feelings of others.

193

The Rising Sign, also known as the Ascendant, is the zodiac sign that was rising on the eastern horizon at the time of a person's birth. It governs one's outward demeanor, appearance, and the first impression they make on others. The Rising Sign represents the mask we wear to the world and how we approach new situations. It can influence how others perceive us and how we navigate social interactions. For instance, someone with a Rising Sign in Scorpio may come across as intense, mysterious, and deeply perceptive.

When these three key elements – the Sun, Moon, and Rising Signs – are combined and analyzed together, a more holistic understanding of an individual's personality emerges. By looking at how these signs interact and influence each other, astrologers can uncover deeper layers of the psyche, motivations, and potential challenges and opportunities in a person's life.

For example, a person with a Sun in Aries, Moon in Cancer, and a Taurus Rising may exhibit a combination of assertiveness, emotional sensitivity, and a grounded, practical approach to life. This individual may have a strong drive for independence and leadership (Aries Sun), a nurturing and protective instinct towards loved ones (Cancer Moon), and a calm and steady demeanor in social settings (Taurus Rising).

In conclusion, combining the Sun, Moon, and Rising Signs in astrology provides a comprehensive framework for understanding the complexities of an individual's personality, emotions, and life path. By delving into how these elements interact and influence each other, we can gain valuable insights into our strengths, weaknesses, and the unique ways in which we navigate the world around us.

Integrating Astrological Insights into Your Life

Integrating astrological insights into your life involves using the knowledge gained from your birth chart and understanding of your zodiac sign to enhance various aspects of your life. By incorporating astrology into your daily routine, decision-making process, relationships, and personal growth journey, you can leverage this ancient wisdom to lead a more fulfilling and purposeful life.

One of the key ways to integrate astrological insights into your life is by aligning your daily routine with the characteristics and tendencies of your zodiac sign. Understanding your strengths and weaknesses as determined by your astrological profile can help you structure your day in a way that maximizes productivity and well-being. For example, if you are a Virgo, known for being detail-oriented and organized, you may thrive in a structured environment with clear goals and tasks to accomplish each day.

Astrology can also provide valuable guidance in decision-making processes. By consulting your birth chart or seeking advice from an astrologer, you can gain clarity on important life choices such as career changes, relationships, or personal development goals. For instance, if you are a Libra facing a career crossroads, you may benefit from understanding how your zodiac sign influences your decision-making style and preferences for a harmonious work environment.

In relationships, integrating astrological insights can lead to deeper understanding and compatibility with others. By exploring the dynamics of zodiac sign compatibility, you can enhance your communication skills, empathy, and ability to navigate conflicts effectively. Whether in romantic partnerships, friendships, or family relationships, astrology can offer insights into personality traits, emotional needs, and potential areas of growth for both yourself and others.

Furthermore, astrology can be a powerful tool for personal growth and self-awareness. By delving into the deeper meanings of your zodiac sign, planetary influences, and aspects of your birth chart, you can uncover hidden talents, challenges, and opportunities for growth. This self-reflection process can help you set meaningful goals, overcome obstacles, and embrace your full potential with confidence and purpose.

Integrating astrological insights into your life also involves recognizing the cyclical nature of planetary movements and their impact on your experiences. By staying attuned to astrological events such as retrogrades, eclipses, and transits, you can better understand the energies at play in your life and make informed choices accordingly. This awareness can help you navigate challenges, seize opportunities, and cultivate a sense of balance and alignment with the cosmic forces at work.

In conclusion, integrating astrological insights into your life is a holistic approach to self-discovery, personal development, and meaningful living. By incorporating astrology into your daily routines, decision-making processes, relationships, and personal growth journey, you can harness the wisdom of the stars to illuminate your path and empower yourself to create a life that resonates with your true essence and purpose.

Made in the USA
Las Vegas, NV
23 December 2024

15267350R00107